very Short Introduction

VERY SHORT INTRODUCTIONS are for anyone wanting a stimulating and accessible way into a new subject. They are written by experts, and have been translated into more than 40 different languages.

The series began in 1995, and now covers a wide variety of topics in every discipline. The VSI library now contains over 350 volumes—a Very Short Introduction to everything from Psychology and Philosophy of Science to American History and Relativity—and continues to grow in every subject area.

Very Short Introductions available now:

ACCOUNTING Christopher Nobes
ADVERTISING Winston Fletcher
AFRICAN AMERICAN RELIGION
Eddie S. Glaude Jr.
AFRICAN HISTORY John Parker and
Richard Rathbone
AFRICAN RELIGIONS
Jacob K. Olupona
AGNOSTICISM Robin Le Poidevin
ALEXANDER THE GREAT
Hugh Bowden
AMERICAN HISTORY Paul S. Boyer
AMERICAN IMMIGRATION
David A. Gerber
AMERICAN LEGAL HISTORY
G. Edward White
AMERICAN POLITICAL HISTORY
Donald Critchlow
AMERICAN POLITICAL PARTIES
AND ELECTIONS L. Sandy Maisel
AMERICAN POLITICS
Richard M. Valelly
THE AMERICAN PRESIDENCY
Charles O. Jones
AMERICAN SLAVERY
Heather Andrea Williams
THE AMERICAN WEST Stephen Aron
AMERICAN WOMEN'S HISTORY
Susan Ware
ANAESTHESIA Aidan O'Donnell
ANARCHISM Colin Ward
ANCIENT EGYPT Ian Shaw
ANCIENT EGYPTIAN ART AND
ARCHITECTURE Christina Riggs
ANCIENT GREECE Paul Cartledge

THE ANCIENT NEAR EAST
Amanda H. Podany
ANCIENT PHILOSOPHY Julia Annas
ANCIENT WARFARE
Harry Sidebottom
ANGELS David Albert Jones
ANGLICANISM Mark Chapman
THE ANGLO-SAXON AGE John Blair
THE ANIMAL KINGDOM
Peter Holland
ANIMAL RIGHTS David DeGrazia
THE ANTARCTIC Klaus Dodds
ANTISEMITISM Steven Beller
ANXIETY Daniel Freeman and
Jason Freeman
THE APOCRYPHAL GOSPELS
Paul Foster
ARCHAEOLOGY Paul Bahn
ARCHITECTURE Andrew Ballantyne
ARISTOCRACY William Doyle
ARISTOTLE Jonathan Barnes
ART HISTORY Dana Arnold
ART THEORY Cynthia Freeland
ASTROBIOLOGY David C. Catling
ATHEISM Julian Baggini
AUGUSTINE Henry Chadwick
AUSTRALIA Kenneth Morgan
AUTISM Uta Frith
THE AVANT GARDE David Cottington
THE AZTECS David Carrasco
BACTERIA Sebastian G. B. Amyes
BARTHES Jonathan Culler
THE BEATS David Sterritt
BEAUTY Roger Scruton
BESTSELLERS John Sutherland

THE BIBLE John Riches
BIBLICAL ARCHAEOLOGY
    Eric H. Cline
BIOGRAPHY Hermione Lee
THE BLUES Elijah Wald
THE BOOK OF MORMON Terryl Givens
BORDERS Alexander C. Diener and
    Joshua Hagen
THE BRAIN Michael O'Shea
THE BRITISH CONSTITUTION
    Martin Loughlin
THE BRITISH EMPIRE Ashley Jackson
BRITISH POLITICS Anthony Wright
BUDDHA Michael Carrithers
BUDDHISM Damien Keown
BUDDHIST ETHICS Damien Keown
CANCER Nicholas James
CAPITALISM James Fulcher
CATHOLICISM Gerald O'Collins
CAUSATION Stephen Mumford and
    Rani Lill Anjum
THE CELL Terence Allen and
    Graham Cowling
THE CELTS Barry Cunliffe
CHAOS Leonard Smith
CHEMISTRY Peter Atkins
CHILDREN'S LITERATURE
    Kimberley Reynolds
CHILD PSYCHOLOGY Usha Goswami
CHINESE LITERATURE Sabina Knight
CHOICE THEORY Michael Allingham
CHRISTIAN ART Beth Williamson
CHRISTIAN ETHICS D. Stephen Long
CHRISTIANITY Linda Woodhead
CITIZENSHIP Richard Bellamy
CIVIL ENGINEERING
    David Muir Wood
CLASSICAL LITERATURE William Allan
CLASSICAL MYTHOLOGY
    Helen Morales
CLASSICS Mary Beard and
    John Henderson
CLAUSEWITZ Michael Howard
CLIMATE Mark Maslin
THE COLD WAR Robert McMahon
COLONIAL AMERICA Alan Taylor
COLONIAL LATIN AMERICAN
    LITERATURE Rolena Adorno
COMEDY Matthew Bevis
COMMUNISM Leslie Holmes
COMPLEXITY John H. Holland

THE COMPUTER Darrel Ince
CONFUCIANISM Daniel K. Gardner
THE CONQUISTADORS
    Matthew Restall and
    Felipe Fernández-Armesto
CONSCIENCE Paul Strohm
CONSCIOUSNESS Susan Blackmore
CONTEMPORARY ART
    Julian Stallabrass
CONTEMPORARY FICTION
    Robert Eaglestone
CONTINENTAL PHILOSOPHY
    Simon Critchley
CORAL REEFS Charles Sheppard
CORPORATE SOCIAL RESPONSIBILITY
    Jeremy Moon
COSMOLOGY Peter Coles
CRITICAL THEORY
    Stephen Eric Bronner
THE CRUSADES Christopher Tyerman
CRYPTOGRAPHY Fred Piper and
    Sean Murphy
THE CULTURAL REVOLUTION
    Richard Curt Kraus
DADA AND SURREALISM
    David Hopkins
DANTE Peter Hainsworth and
    David Robey
DARWIN Jonathan Howard
THE DEAD SEA SCROLLS Timothy Lim
DEMOCRACY Bernard Crick
DERRIDA Simon Glendinning
DESCARTES Tom Sorell
DESERTS Nick Middleton
DESIGN John Heskett
DEVELOPMENTAL BIOLOGY
    Lewis Wolpert
THE DEVIL Darren Oldridge
DIASPORA Kevin Kenny
DICTIONARIES Lynda Mugglestone
DINOSAURS David Norman
DIPLOMACY Joseph M. Siracusa
DOCUMENTARY FILM
    Patricia Aufderheide
DREAMING J. Allan Hobson
DRUGS Leslie Iversen
DRUIDS Barry Cunliffe
EARLY MUSIC Thomas Forrest Kelly
THE EARTH Martin Redfern
ECONOMICS Partha Dasgupta
EDUCATION Gary Thomas

EGYPTIAN MYTH Geraldine Pinch
EIGHTEENTH-CENTURY BRITAIN
    Paul Langford
THE ELEMENTS Philip Ball
EMOTION Dylan Evans
EMPIRE Stephen Howe
ENGELS Terrell Carver
ENGINEERING David Blockley
ENGLISH LITERATURE Jonathan Bate
ENTREPRENEURSHIP Paul Westhead
    and Mike Wright
ENVIRONMENTAL ECONOMICS
    Stephen Smith
EPIDEMIOLOGY Rodolfo Saracci
ETHICS Simon Blackburn
ETHNOMUSICOLOGY Timothy Rice
THE ETRUSCANS Christopher Smith
THE EUROPEAN UNION John Pinder
    and Simon Usherwood
EVOLUTION Brian and
    Deborah Charlesworth
EXISTENTIALISM Thomas Flynn
EXPLORATION Stewart A. Weaver
THE EYE Michael Land
FAMILY LAW Jonathan Herring
FASCISM Kevin Passmore
FASHION Rebecca Arnold
FEMINISM Margaret Walters
FILM Michael Wood
FILM MUSIC Kathryn Kalinak
THE FIRST WORLD WAR
    Michael Howard
FOLK MUSIC Mark Slobin
FOOD John Krebs
FORENSIC PSYCHOLOGY
    David Canter
FORENSIC SCIENCE Jim Fraser
FOSSILS Keith Thomson
FOUCAULT Gary Gutting
FRACTALS Kenneth Falconer
FREE SPEECH Nigel Warburton
FREE WILL Thomas Pink
FRENCH LITERATURE John D. Lyons
THE FRENCH REVOLUTION
    William Doyle
FREUD Anthony Storr
FUNDAMENTALISM Malise Ruthven
GALAXIES John Gribbin
GALILEO Stillman Drake
GAME THEORY Ken Binmore
GANDHI Bhikhu Parekh

GENES Jonathan Slack
GENIUS Andrew Robinson
GEOGRAPHY John Matthews and
    David Herbert
GEOPOLITICS Klaus Dodds
GERMAN LITERATURE Nicholas Boyle
GERMAN PHILOSOPHY
    Andrew Bowie
GLOBAL CATASTROPHES Bill McGuire
GLOBAL ECONOMIC HISTORY
    Robert C. Allen
GLOBALIZATION Manfred Steger
GOD John Bowker
THE GOTHIC Nick Groom
GOVERNANCE Mark Bevir
THE GREAT DEPRESSION AND THE
    NEW DEAL Eric Rauchway
HABERMAS James Gordon Finlayson
HAPPINESS Daniel M. Haybron
HEGEL Peter Singer
HEIDEGGER Michael Inwood
HERODOTUS Jennifer T. Roberts
HIEROGLYPHS Penelope Wilson
HINDUISM Kim Knott
HISTORY John H. Arnold
THE HISTORY OF ASTRONOMY
    Michael Hoskin
THE HISTORY OF LIFE
    Michael Benton
THE HISTORY OF MATHEMATICS
    Jacqueline Stedall
THE HISTORY OF MEDICINE
    William Bynum
THE HISTORY OF TIME
    Leofranc Holford-Strevens
HIV/AIDS Alan Whiteside
HOBBES Richard Tuck
HORMONES Martin Luck
HUMAN ANATOMY
    Leslie Klenerman
HUMAN EVOLUTION Bernard Wood
HUMAN RIGHTS Andrew Clapham
HUMANISM Stephen Law
HUME A. J. Ayer
HUMOUR Noël Carroll
THE ICE AGE Jamie Woodward
IDEOLOGY Michael Freeden
INDIAN PHILOSOPHY Sue Hamilton
INFORMATION Luciano Floridi
INNOVATION Mark Dodgson and
    David Gann

INTELLIGENCE Ian J. Deary
INTERNATIONAL MIGRATION
   Khalid Koser
INTERNATIONAL RELATIONS
   Paul Wilkinson
INTERNATIONAL SECURITY
   Christopher S. Browning
IRAN Ali M. Ansari
ISLAM Malise Ruthven
ISLAMIC HISTORY Adam Silverstein
ITALIAN LITERATURE
   Peter Hainsworth and
   David Robey
JESUS Richard Bauckham
JOURNALISM Ian Hargreaves
JUDAISM Norman Solomon
JUNG Anthony Stevens
KABBALAH Joseph Dan
KAFKA Ritchie Robertson
KANT Roger Scruton
KEYNES Robert Skidelsky
KIERKEGAARD Patrick Gardiner
KNOWLEDGE Jennifer Nagel
THE KORAN Michael Cook
LANDSCAPE ARCHITECTURE
   Ian H. Thompson
LANDSCAPES AND
   GEOMORPHOLOGY
   Andrew Goudie and Heather Viles
LANGUAGES Stephen R. Anderson
LATE ANTIQUITY Gillian Clark
LAW Raymond Wacks
THE LAWS OF THERMODYNAMICS
   Peter Atkins
LEADERSHIP Keith Grint
LINCOLN Allen C. Guelzo
LINGUISTICS Peter Matthews
LITERARY THEORY Jonathan Culler
LOCKE John Dunn
LOGIC Graham Priest
LOVE Ronald de Sousa
MACHIAVELLI Quentin Skinner
MADNESS Andrew Scull
MAGIC Owen Davies
MAGNA CARTA Nicholas Vincent
MAGNETISM Stephen Blundell
MALTHUS Donald Winch
MANAGEMENT John Hendry
MAO Delia Davin
MARINE BIOLOGY Philip V. Mladenov
THE MARQUIS DE SADE John Phillips

MARTIN LUTHER Scott H. Hendrix
MARTYRDOM Jolyon Mitchell
MARX Peter Singer
MATERIALS Christopher Hall
MATHEMATICS Timothy Gowers
THE MEANING OF LIFE
   Terry Eagleton
MEDICAL ETHICS Tony Hope
MEDICAL LAW Charles Foster
MEDIEVAL BRITAIN John Gillingham
   and Ralph A. Griffiths
MEMORY Jonathan K. Foster
METAPHYSICS Stephen Mumford
MICHAEL FARADAY
   Frank A. J. L. James
MICROBIOLOGY Nicholas P. Money
MICROECONOMICS Avinash Dixit
THE MIDDLE AGES Miri Rubin
MINERALS David Vaughan
MODERN ART David Cottington
MODERN CHINA Rana Mitter
MODERN FRANCE
   Vanessa R. Schwartz
MODERN IRELAND Senia Pašeta
MODERN JAPAN
   Christopher Goto-Jones
MODERN LATIN AMERICAN
   LITERATURE
   Roberto González Echevarría
MODERN WAR Richard English
MODERNISM Christopher Butler
MOLECULES Philip Ball
THE MONGOLS Morris Rossabi
MORMONISM
   Richard Lyman Bushman
MUHAMMAD Jonathan A. C. Brown
MULTICULTURALISM Ali Rattansi
MUSIC Nicholas Cook
MYTH Robert A. Segal
THE NAPOLEONIC WARS
   Mike Rapport
NATIONALISM Steven Grosby
NELSON MANDELA Elleke Boehmer
NEOLIBERALISM Manfred Steger and
   Ravi Roy
NETWORKS Guido Caldarelli and
   Michele Catanzaro
THE NEW TESTAMENT
   Luke Timothy Johnson
THE NEW TESTAMENT AS
   LITERATURE Kyle Keefer

NEWTON Robert Iliffe
NIETZSCHE Michael Tanner
NINETEENTH-CENTURY BRITAIN
  Christopher Harvie and
  H. C. G. Matthew
THE NORMAN CONQUEST
  George Garnett
NORTH AMERICAN INDIANS
  Theda Perdue and Michael D. Green
NORTHERN IRELAND
  Marc Mulholland
NOTHING Frank Close
NUCLEAR POWER Maxwell Irvine
NUCLEAR WEAPONS
  Joseph M. Siracusa
NUMBERS Peter M. Higgins
NUTRITION David A. Bender
OBJECTIVITY Stephen Gaukroger
THE OLD TESTAMENT
  Michael D. Coogan
THE ORCHESTRA D. Kern Holoman
ORGANIZATIONS Mary Jo Hatch
PAGANISM Owen Davies
THE PALESTINIAN-ISRAELI CONFLICT
  Martin Bunton
PARTICLE PHYSICS Frank Close
PAUL E. P. Sanders
PEACE Oliver P. Richmond
PENTECOSTALISM William K. Kay
THE PERIODIC TABLE Eric R. Scerri
PHILOSOPHY Edward Craig
PHILOSOPHY OF LAW
  Raymond Wacks
PHILOSOPHY OF SCIENCE
  Samir Okasha
PHOTOGRAPHY Steve Edwards
PHYSICAL CHEMISTRY Peter Atkins
PLAGUE Paul Slack
PLANETS David A. Rothery
PLANTS Timothy Walker
PLATO Julia Annas
POLITICAL PHILOSOPHY David Miller
POLITICS Kenneth Minogue
POSTCOLONIALISM Robert Young
POSTMODERNISM Christopher Butler
POSTSTRUCTURALISM
  Catherine Belsey
PREHISTORY Chris Gosden
PRESOCRATIC PHILOSOPHY
  Catherine Osborne

PRIVACY Raymond Wacks
PROBABILITY John Haigh
PROGRESSIVISM Walter Nugent
PROTESTANTISM Mark A. Noll
PSYCHIATRY Tom Burns
PSYCHOLOGY Gillian Butler and
  Freda McManus
PSYCHOTHERAPY Tom Burns and
  Eva Burns-Lundgren
PURITANISM Francis J. Bremer
THE QUAKERS Pink Dandelion
QUANTUM THEORY
  John Polkinghorne
RACISM Ali Rattansi
RADIOACTIVITY Claudio Tuniz
RASTAFARI Ennis B. Edmonds
THE REAGAN REVOLUTION Gil Troy
REALITY Jan Westerhoff
THE REFORMATION Peter Marshall
RELATIVITY Russell Stannard
RELIGION IN AMERICA Timothy Beal
THE RENAISSANCE Jerry Brotton
RENAISSANCE ART
  Geraldine A. Johnson
REVOLUTIONS Jack A. Goldstone
RHETORIC Richard Toye
RISK Baruch Fischhoff and
  John Kadvany
RITUAL Barry Stephenson
RIVERS Nick Middleton
ROBOTICS Alan Winfield
ROMAN BRITAIN Peter Salway
THE ROMAN EMPIRE
  Christopher Kelly
THE ROMAN REPUBLIC
  David M. Gwynn
ROMANTICISM Michael Ferber
ROUSSEAU Robert Wokler
RUSSELL A. C. Grayling
RUSSIAN HISTORY Geoffrey Hosking
RUSSIAN LITERATURE Catriona Kelly
THE RUSSIAN REVOLUTION
  S. A. Smith
SCHIZOPHRENIA Chris Frith and
  Eve Johnstone
SCHOPENHAUER
  Christopher Janaway
SCIENCE AND RELIGION
  Thomas Dixon
SCIENCE FICTION David Seed

THE SCIENTIFIC REVOLUTION
  Lawrence M. Principe
SCOTLAND Rab Houston
SEXUALITY Véronique Mottier
SHAKESPEARE Germaine Greer
SIKHISM Eleanor Nesbitt
THE SILK ROAD James A. Millward
SLEEP Steven W. Lockley and
  Russell G. Foster
SOCIAL AND CULTURAL
  ANTHROPOLOGY
  John Monaghan and Peter Just
SOCIALISM Michael Newman
SOCIOLINGUISTICS John Edwards
SOCIOLOGY Steve Bruce
SOCRATES C. C. W. Taylor
THE SOVIET UNION Stephen Lovell
THE SPANISH CIVIL WAR
  Helen Graham
SPANISH LITERATURE Jo Labanyi
SPINOZA Roger Scruton
SPIRITUALITY Philip Sheldrake
SPORT Mike Cronin
STARS Andrew King
STATISTICS David J. Hand
STEM CELLS Jonathan Slack
STRUCTURAL ENGINEERING
  David Blockley
STUART BRITAIN John Morrill
SUPERCONDUCTIVITY
  Stephen Blundell
SYMMETRY Ian Stewart

TEETH Peter S. Ungar
TERRORISM Charles Townshend
THEATRE Marvin Carlson
THEOLOGY David F. Ford
THOMAS AQUINAS Fergus Kerr
THOUGHT Tim Bayne
TIBETAN BUDDHISM
  Matthew T. Kapstein
TOCQUEVILLE Harvey C. Mansfield
TRAGEDY Adrian Poole
THE TROJAN WAR Eric H. Cline
TRUST Katherine Hawley
THE TUDORS John Guy
TWENTIETH-CENTURY BRITAIN
  Kenneth O. Morgan
THE UNITED NATIONS
  Jussi M. Hanhimäki
THE U.S. CONGRESS Donald A. Ritchie
THE U.S. SUPREME COURT
  Linda Greenhouse
UTOPIANISM Lyman Tower Sargent
THE VIKINGS Julian Richards
VIRUSES Dorothy H. Crawford
WITCHCRAFT Malcolm Gaskill
WITTGENSTEIN A. C. Grayling
WORK Stephen Fineman
WORLD MUSIC Philip Bohlman
THE WORLD TRADE
  ORGANIZATION Amrita Narlikar
WORLD WAR II Gerhard L. Weinberg
WRITING AND SCRIPT
  Andrew Robinson

Available soon:

PLATE TECTONICS Peter Molnar
ANCIENT ASSYRIA Karen Radner
TAXATION Stephen Smith

CORRUPTION Leslie Holmes
PILGRIMAGE Ian Reader

For more information visit our website

www.oup.com/vsi/

Peter Hainsworth and David Robey

DANTE

A Very Short Introduction

OXFORD
UNIVERSITY PRESS

OXFORD
UNIVERSITY PRESS

Great Clarendon Street, Oxford, OX2 6DP,
United Kingdom

Oxford University Press is a department of the University of Oxford.
It furthers the University's objective of excellence in research, scholarship,
and education by publishing worldwide. Oxford is a registered trade mark of
Oxford University Press in the UK and in certain other countries

© Peter Hainsworth and David Robey 2015

The moral rights of the authors have been asserted

First edition published in 2015

Impression: 5

Published in the United States of America by Oxford University Press
198 Madison Avenue, New York, NY 10016, United States of America

British Library Cataloguing in Publication Data

Data available

Library of Congress Control Number: 2014949661

ISBN 978-0-19-968477-9

Printed in Great Britain by
Ashford Colour Press Ltd, Gosport, Hampshire

Contents

List of illustrations xiii

Note to reader xv

1 Introduction 1

2 Autobiography 11

3 Truth 29

4 Writing 44

5 Humanity 65

6 Politics 84

7 God 99

Further reading 116

Index 119

List of illustrations

1 Ulysses (*Inferno* 26) **4**

The Bodleian Libraries,
The University of Oxford,
MS Holkham Misc. 48, p. 40

2 John Batten, Dante
recognizing Brunetto Latini
(*Inferno* 15) **6**

Image courtesy of the Principal
and Fellows of Lady Margaret
Hall, Oxford for permission to
reproduce the image

3 Portrait of Dante by Giovanni
del Ponte (15th century) **12**

© 2014. Photo Scala, Florence—
courtesy of the Biblioteca Riccardiana

4 General map of the
Afterworld **31**

Wikimedia Commons/Public Domain

5 Dante Gabriel Rossetti,
Beatrice Meeting Dante at a
Wedding Feast **49**

The Art Archive/Ashmolean Museum

6 Roberto Benigni reciting
Dante **58**

Image by © New Press Photo/Splash
News/Corbis

7 Alberto Martini, Ugolino and
the Archbishop Ruggieri
(*Inferno* 33) **77**

The Art Archive/Fondazione Oderzo
Cultura, Oderzo/Mondadori
Portfolio/Electa

8 Gustave Doré, The
Whore and the Giant
(*Purgatorio* 33) **95**

© 2014. White Images/Scala,
Florence

9 Sandro Botticelli,
The River of Light
(*Paradiso* 30) **113**

bpk/Kupferstichkabinett,
Staatliche Museen zu Berlin/
Philipp Allard

Note to reader

Except for the *Divine Comedy*, we use the customary Italian or Latin titles for Dante's works and discuss their significance at appropriate moments.

References to the *Comedy* are by *cantica* (the three major divisions: *Inferno*, *Purgatorio*, and *Paradiso*), canto, and line number(s): e.g. *Inf.* 21.139. All translations of quotations are our own and aim to be literal rather than elegant.

References to the *Rime* follow Contini's numbering (see Further reading).

The lists of figures in Boxes 3–5 include only those we mention or discuss elsewhere.

References use the following abbreviations:

Inf.	*Inferno*
Purg.	*Purgatorio*
Par.	*Paradiso*
VN	*Vita nova*
Conv.	*Convivio*
Mon.	*Monarchia*
DVE	*De vulgari eloquentia*
Ep.	*Epistles*

Chapter 1
Introduction

Fatti non foste a viver come bruti
ma per seguir virtute e canoscenza
[You were not made to live like brute beasts,
but to pursue virtue and knowledge]

(*Inf.* 26.119–20)

Ulysses and Brunetto

The lines are some of the most famous in the *Divine Comedy*. Energetic, compressed, assured, and, in the original, immediately memorable, they urge us to embrace the capacities that our human nature offers and live them to the full, not just for private satisfaction, but to acquire both moral virtue and knowledge of the world. It is a vision of what human life should be, which Dante took from classical philosophy and which he repeatedly affirms. It will be at the heart of the Italian Renaissance and is still a vital element of Western culture today. In *If this be a man* Primo Levi recounts that it was these lines that he recalled at one of his worst moments in Auschwitz, and no wonder, for it was precisely what these lines are saying that Nazism was set on destroying.

In canto 26 of the *Comedy* Dante speaks these lines through the mouth of Ulysses, the Homeric hero of the Trojan war, who devised the stratagem of the Wooden Horse, and, after Troy fell, lived through ten years of adventures across the Mediterranean before arriving back at his home island of Ithaca. His reunion with his wife Penelope and his son is where Homer brings the story to an end. It is where Dante, who did not know Homer but knew the story from other sources, has his Ulysses begin. Love of his family could not keep him, he says, from wanting to see and learn more of the world. When he reaches the western limits of the Mediterranean with the now ageing crew of his remaining boat, he inspires them with the stirring speech from which the two lines are taken, and they sail on south-west beyond the equator into an empty ocean. To their delight they eventually see a mountain rising in the distance, but they never reach land. From the mountain comes a sudden whirlwind which spins their ship round and sinks it. There the account ends.

It is a heroic voyage, if a doomed one. Dante's Ulysses is a prototype for many a modern hero setting out to explore the unknown and face destiny. He is also in a sense Dante: a younger Dante, perhaps, with an enthusiasm for human knowledge later viewed as excessive by the poet of the *Comedy*; and perhaps also the older exile and wanderer, tenaciously holding on to his values in a hostile world. It is not just moderns who see the parallel. Petrarch, writing about forty years after Dante's death, quotes directly from Ulysses' speech to characterize Dante's poetic and personal resolve. In the *Comedy* Dante himself returns at various points to the voyage, suggesting possible contrasts and comparisons with his own unprecedented journey. Like Ulysses Dante journeys into a 'world without people' (*Inf.* 26.117), in his case the world of the dead. But he explicitly emphasizes crucial differences. His journey is divinely authorized, and it leads to intellectual, moral, and spiritual enlightenment, whereas Ulysses goes off on a 'mad flight' (l.125). The nameless mountain Ulysses saw is Purgatory, which Dante will climb in the second part of his poem and ascend from there into the Heavens. Ulysses is one of the damned, condemned to hell for committing the sin of false counsel during the Trojan war; his punishment for this abuse of the tongue is to be enveloped for ever in a double-tongued flame together with Diomedes, his partner in crime, who for Homer was one of the great Greek heroes. Yet the punishment makes him if anything more imposing. All the souls in Hell inhabit a simulacrum of their human body, but Ulysses' is hidden, and his voice seems to come from a remote, heroic past. Appropriately, Dante cannot address him directly; Virgil, the Roman poet and Dante's guide through Hell and Purgatory, has to act as intermediary (see Figure 1).

Is the heroic journey Ulysses makes a mistake? Is his speech to his crew really another example of false counsel? Are Dante's underlying worries about his own enterprise coming through? Or alternatively is there an admiration which his severe Christian judgement cannot repress? Readers have responded in different ways to these unavoidable questions and a great many pages have been written about them. No one has come up with definitive answers, and that is part of Dante's greatness. The Ulysses episode impresses us with its force and energy, its graphic qualities and emotional power, but here and elsewhere Dante refuses to let us settle for a purely emotional and imaginative response or for a simple moralizing reading. Sin is ambiguous and multifaceted and the sinner may have virtues as well as faults. Dante draws us into the complex business of judgement; his characters do not merely exemplify a doctrine.

Ulysses is one of many well-known figures from antiquity that Dante the character encounters in the course of his journey, some mythical like Ulysses, others historical, such as his guide Virgil. One of the *Comedy*'s striking novelties is to juxtapose figures like these with others from the 12th and 13th centuries. Some are or were famous politicians, poets, or intellectuals. Others are barely known outside Dante's work, the outstanding example being his beloved Beatrice, who will replace Virgil and guide him to the summit of Paradise. There are other souls of people he knew personally. It is often said that he put his enemies in Hell to take

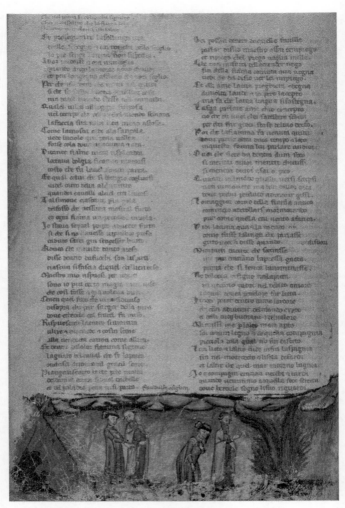

1. Ulysses (*Inferno* 26). In this 14th century manuscript illustration, Virgil and Dante speak before Virgil moves forward to address Ulysses, who is enveloped in the double-tongued flame with Diomedes, while Dante bows reverently behind him.

revenge on them. This is arguably so in a few cases, but by no means all. As with Ulysses, on various occasions there is anything but enmity in play, and Dante's representation is notable as much for the questions that it raises as for the judgement that is expressed.

Earlier in *Inferno*, in canto 15, Dante and Virgil walk along a raised embankment above a desert of burning sand, onto which flakes of fire rain down from above. A troop of souls passes on the sand and gazes at Dante and his guide, in the way, Dante says, that passers-by peer at each other in the moonlight (Hell is dark). One of them tugs at Dante's cloak with an expression of astonishment, and with equal astonishment, under the burnt features, Dante recognizes his friend and occasional mentor, Brunetto Latini: 'Siete voi qui, ser Brunetto?' (l. 30: 'Are you *here*, Master Brunetto?'), his use of the polite 'voi' form and the title 'ser' indicating his respect. There follows a particularly intense and personal encounter (see Figure 2).

Brunetto Latini died in 1293, a little over six years before the purported date of Dante's journey through the next world at Easter 1300. He was a leading Florentine citizen, a civic official, and a well-known writer, who was a significant figure in the development of Florentine civic culture. His major work, *Li Livres dou tresor* (*The Book of Treasure*), is an encyclopaedic and highly derivative compendium written in French during a period of exile. It covers most branches of contemporary knowledge, with a particular focus on ethics, rhetoric, and politics. Anticipating the Florentine Renaissance of the 15th century, it promotes the classical Latin view of the importance for good government of the arts of expression and argument. During their conversation Dante recalls Brunetto's 'dear and good fatherly image' (*Inf.* 15.82), and says that he taught him 'how man makes himself eternal' (ll. 83–5). We do not know whether Brunetto actually gave Dante any tuition when he was a young man; here it is more likely that he has Brunetto's general ethical, political, and rhetorical

2. John Batten, Dante recognizing Brunetto Latini (*Inferno* 15). In this early 20th century drawing, Brunetto is unusually youthful, Dante wears the hood he has in most images, and Virgil is, as often, a pensive sage.

influence in mind. At the end of the episode Brunetto recommends his *Tresor* 'in which I still live' to Dante (l. 120): he made himself eternal not in the next world but in the life above, through his writings, and perhaps through his civic activity. If this neglect of life in the next world was wrong, Dante's admiration for Brunetto is clear in his reverent attitude throughout the episode, the dignity and pathos with which his old mentor speaks, and the striking image with which the canto concludes: as Brunetto runs off to rejoin his group of sinners, Dante compares him to a runner in the Veronese *palio*, and one who is winning, not losing (ll. 121–4).

The encounter takes place in the circle of the violent, in the section where those who were violent against nature are punished. Brunetto is guilty of the sin of Sodom, or homosexuality, which, following the common assumption of his time and many centuries

6

thereafter, Dante considers not only an offence against nature but also exclusively male. Running for all eternity in groups across the burning sand connotes the supposed emptiness, aridity, and futility of homosexual love. Nevertheless it is not for the mere sin of sodomy that Brunetto is damned, but because, like all the sinners in Hell, he did not repent before he died. If he had, he would have been accorded God's grace, and after an appropriate period of penance in Purgatory eventually entered Paradise.

Dante's harsh treatment of unrepentant homosexuals is integrally related to the fundamental elements of his vision. Violence against nature is located in the same section of Hell as violence against God, i.e. blasphemy, and also usury: lending money at interest is an offence against both God and nature because it makes money something other than the just reward of labour. Human beings must love God and follow the natural order in their work as well as in their sexual behaviour. Nature is God's creation and the material embodiment of the divine mind: with man at its centre, created in God's image, the whole universe possesses an order which makes it similar to God, and is ruled by God through that order. In *Inferno* the focus is on the consequences of infringing the divine order, while a positive vision of what it is will be laid out in *Paradiso*. Reading the *Comedy* requires coming to terms not just with Dante's views on morality, but with the comprehensive metaphysical and theological system that underpins them. The system, and Dante's progressive understanding of it, is a large part of what the poem is about.

In the Brunetto episode Dante seems to put great emphasis on human factors, and to heighten and complicate the tensions between them and the divine system. There is no other evidence beyond what he says here that Brunetto was in reality a homosexual, but whether he was or not, Dante has chosen to suggest the complex individuality of his former teacher and to foreground in their encounter personal issues of central importance to him. Dante has Brunetto comment fiercely on the current deplorable state of his native Florence, and predict his own coming banishment, which will lead eventually to his glorious destiny as a poet. This poetic career is seen as indebted in some fundamental way to Brunetto and the literary ethos he represents, associated as he is with other men of letters of the same classical bent. Much more than with Ulysses, we are plunged here into the reality of Florentine politics and culture as well as of Dante's personal experience as a prominent and active politician before his exile. Not only that, but the encounter itself has the qualities of a real meeting: a pupil unexpectedly encountering his old teacher and talking with him about the past and future at a point when they have both, for better and worse, moved on. It is a powerfully moving moment for Dante and for the reader, the earthly emotions and the vividness accented by the succinct comparisons, especially the final image of Brunetto looking like a winner, when we know that in fact he is a loser par excellence.

Dante modern and medieval

These quite different episodes are two of the most striking illustrations of the tension that runs all the way through the *Comedy* between the human and the divine, and the modern and the medieval. Dante speaks in so many ways to the present; at the same time, as many have observed, his work is also a vast synthesis or *summa* of later medieval culture. Readers accustomed to the idea of an expanding universe and humanity as the product of evolution may well find it hard to empathize with Dante's vision, so vigorously stated, of a universe ruled by divine providence and of man created in God's image. Yet at the very least, even if some of the answers he proposes may now seem superannuated, the questions he raises are perennial ones: what is the meaning and purpose of the universe? what is unique and valuable in human beings? why does the experience of love seem transcendental? why is the world in such a bad state? A full reading of Dante requires attention both to its timeless, accessible, and engaging elements, and to its historical particularity. If we neglect one aspect for the other, we greatly reduce the richness, complexity, and range of his extraordinary poem.

These tensions will remain a guiding consideration in the chapters that follow, each of which takes up a topic or theme raised in either the Ulysses or the Brunetto episode or both. Each of these is part of our modern discourse and central to Dante's work as well, but understood by him in many respects, as we shall see, quite differently from the way in which we understand them today. It has to be said, however, that our ideal of a full reading of Dante has not been much followed by readers across the centuries, who have tended to pick and choose among the different parts of the *Comedy*, constructing a Dante to suit their own tastes and prejudices. The first commentators, writing soon after Dante's death, tended to force him into allegorical straitjackets, though they also supplied essential historical information about characters and events and equally essential linguistic clarification. Renaissance readers admired the allegory, but found the descents into low language distasteful by the new standards of classicism; Catholics also found the denunciations of the Church unacceptable. The 18th century, still under the sway of classicism, continued to have reservations about the *Comedy*'s poetic form. Nineteenth century readers, who included some real enthusiasts, had a distinct penchant for the more obviously lyrical and Romantic parts, and tended to see Dante as struggling, titanically but ultimately unsuccessfully, to free himself from the shackles of scholasticism. The Risorgimento saw him as a heroic forerunner of Italian Unification. Modern criticism and scholarship have put the emphasis on Dante's relationship to earlier medieval writing, and sometimes produced a Dante who is at least as difficult as the most complex scholastic philosopher. At the same time in recent decades there has been a renewed and widespread recognition of the daring and originality of Dante's imagination and style. This has led to a flood of new translations, as well as to imitations and rewritings by a host of poets, film-makers, and graphic artists. Partly under the influence of European modernism of the last

9

century, Dante criticism is thus taking increasing account of the novel, unconventional, and challenging ways of writing that can be found in the *Comedy*. In this sense our own reading of Dante is to a degree modernistic, though not, we trust, to the point of anachronism; on the contrary, modernism can help a better historical appreciation of the *Comedy*'s novel, unconventional, and challenging properties for its own time as well as for ours.

There is one leading modernist who, in a rather different way, is an essential reference point for any presentation of the poet to English-speaking readers. T. S. Eliot's *Dante*, first published in 1929 and itself a kind of very short introduction, made the now classic comparison with Shakespeare: 'Dante and Shakespeare divide the modern world between them; there is no third.' Dante explored the depths and heights of human experience, Shakespeare its width and variety. It is a grand claim that few today would make so categorically or in anything like the same terms, though it can still hold to a degree. In contrast, our approach has tended to bring Dante and Shakespeare closer together. The irreducible uncertainties and dramatic tensions that we will highlight in the *Comedy* have their parallels in Shakespeare's plays. Understanding is central to Dante's poetry, and at the same time he resists total intellectual systematization, even if he propels his readers much more in that direction than Shakespeare does. Curiously, for a modernist, Eliot also declared Dante's language to be simple in comparison to Shakespeare's. As we shall try to show, it actually has a complexity, boldness, and inventiveness that makes Dante comparable to Shakespeare in this respect too, for all their differences of period and genre.

Chapter 2
Autobiography

> Non si concede per li rettorici alcuno di sè medesimo sanza
> necessaria cagione parlare
> [It is not permitted by the rhetoricians that anyone should
> speak of himself without just cause]
>
> (*Conv.* 1.2)

Evidence

Dante's works have one recurrent character, Dante himself
(see Figure 3). He is the protagonist of the *Comedy*, the only figure
present from beginning to end of the poem, the traveller through
Hell, Purgatory, and Paradise whose mission is to tell us what he
saw and experienced in the course of his journey, and whose
personality, role, and self-understanding undergo complex
changes as the poem progresses. Dante's first work, the *Vita nova*,
is if anything even more self-focused. A collection of vernacular
lyric poems arranged in chronological order with a linking
commentary, it tells the story of his growth as a poet, and at the
same time of his love for the woman he calls Beatrice, a love which
began suddenly and overwhelmingly when he was 9 years old, he
says, and continued up to and beyond her death on 8 June 1290.
In the early 1300s he starts, but never finishes, the *Convivio*
(or 'Banquet'), a vernacular treatise intended to bring the benefits
of his philosophical reading to an untrained but interested

3. Portrait of Dante by Giovanni del Ponte (15th century). Dante's well-known features derive principally from a description by Boccaccio and become standardized about a hundred years after his death.

readership. It too has a strong personal element: Dante justifies what he is doing partly with reference to the experiences, especially exile from Florence, that have driven him to write. He also claims that some of his poems have been misinterpreted, and are much more serious than superficial readers have judged them

12

to be. The treatise thus takes the unusual form of another self-commentary that aims to justify the poems and bring out their underlying meanings. Around the same time, he starts on another treatise which he will never finish, this time in Latin. In what he completed of the *De vulgari eloquentia* he tries to identify the noblest forms of language and the noblest forms of poetry: the examples are wide-ranging, but it is his own poems drawn from the *Vita nova* and the *Convivio*, plus some uncollected ones, that he particularly instances as corresponding to the theoretical ideals that he formulates. Only three works of any substance have no explicitly personal presence, and the first may well not be by Dante: the early *Fiore*, a summary in the form of a sonnet sequence of the first part of the *Roman de la Rose*; and two late treatises, the *Monarchia*, on the nature and status of imperial government, and the highly scholastic *Quaestio de aqua et terra*, on the geography of the earth.

Dante's particular form of life-writing is not what we expect from modern autobiography. There is no continuous narrative, rather a series of retrospective examinations of phases in his emotional, spiritual, intellectual, and artistic life, with overlaps, shifts of emphasis, and some striking contradictions. Certain topics recur again and again: poems and poetry, Beatrice and love, his evolving reading and thought, and his moral and spiritual progress, which comes most strongly to the fore in the *Comedy*. External or material events figure very little. Of his considerable involvement in Florentine affairs before his exile he wrote nothing, either at the time or later; there are two oblique references to his service as a soldier in the war between Florence and Arezzo in 1289 (*Inf.* 21.95 and 22.1–12), but nothing else (see Box 1). The only event that looms large as a burning personal issue is becoming, as he calls it in his letters, an 'undeserving exile' from Florence in 1302 (*Ep.* 2, 3, 5, 6, 7). The exile itself, which would last the rest of his life, is never dated by him, its circumstances never explained, and the wanderings it led to never detailed. All that we gather from Dante himself is his conviction of having been wrongly banished, his

Box 1 Biography

Florence (1265–1301)

1265	Born
1283?	Association with Guido Cavalcanti (1259?–1300) and other poets of the *dolce stil novo*
1285?	Marries Gemma Donati
1286?	*Fiore* and *Detto d'amore* (if genuine)
1287	In Bologna, perhaps studying
1289	Fights at Campaldino against Aretines
1290	Death of Beatrice
1292–3?	*Vita nova*
Later 1290s	Further love poems
1295–1300	Member of guild of physicians and apothecaries; political activity in Florence
1300	Elected *Priore* for June–August
1301 October	Goes to Rome on embassy to Pope Boniface VIII, never to return
1301 November	Black Guelfs take over in Florence
1302	Condemned to exile

Exile (1302–21)

1306	With the Malaspina family in the Val di Magra in Tuscany
1304–8?	*Convivio* and *De vulgari eloquentia*
1304–19?	Epistles and some further lyric poems
1307?–14?	*Inferno*
1308?–15?	*Purgatorio*
1316?–21	*Paradiso*
1311	In the Casentino in eastern Tuscany
1312–18	Mostly in Verona with Can Grande della Scala
1316?	Letter to Can Grande (if genuine)
1318–19?	*Monarchia*
1318?–21	In Ravenna with Guido Novello da Polenta
1319–20	*Eclogues* to Giovanni del Virgilio
1320	*Quaestio de aqua et terra*
1321	Dies

persistent hope that he might eventually be allowed to return, his rejection of his former political allies, and his relief and gratitude for the moral and material support he was given by various ruling families, especially the Malaspina in the Casentino (*Purg.* 8.112–39), and then more securely the della Scala of Verona (*Par.* 17.70–92).

The gaps and uncertainties are enormous. All the time references in the *Comedy* point to the year Easter 1300 as the date of the journey it narrates. The opening line, 'Nel mezzo del cammin di nostra vita' ('In the middle of the path of our life'), indicates that he was 35 when the journey purportedly took place, given that the *Convivio* locates the mid-point of life at this age; he must therefore have been born in 1265, and from later references we gather it was at the time of year when the sun was in the constellation of Gemini, that is in May or June. The neatness of the pattern and the lack of documentary evidence might cause us at least a flicker of doubt, even if Dante has almost always been taken at his word.

Dante says nothing about his parents, his marriage, his wife, or his children. The one family member he celebrates is his noble 12th century ancestor Cacciaguida, who has a major role in canti 15–17 of *Paradiso*. Dante nowhere says where the family money came from, or how and why he entered Florentine politics, if he was not simply taking on offices in the way that men of the Florentine upper classes regularly did. Of his education he gives us only the hints mentioned in the Brunetto episode, and some remarks in *Convivio* (2.12) about frequenting religious schools after the death of Beatrice, as his interest in philosophy developed. From various remarks and isolated poems he emerges as one of a loose group of poets in Florence, often referred to as the poets of the *dolce stil novo* on the basis of a phrase that he uses of his own work in *Purgatorio* (24.57). Probably he became their leading member, though as a young poet he was less famous than the slightly older and more aristocratic Guido Cavalcanti. He calls the latter his 'primo amico' (first friend) in the *Vita nova*, though there are signs that the friendship foundered on the rocks of intellectual and poetic discord some time before Cavalcanti's death in 1300.

Much of what we know, or think we know, of Dante's life is derived from the commentaries on the *Comedy* that began to appear within a year of his death, the earliest (and most rudimentary) being by his son Jacopo. Subsequent more learned and informative commentators include another son, Pietro, and somewhat later in the 14th century Boccaccio, who inaugurated the still widespread practice of giving lectures on individual canti (later called *lecturae Dantis*), and also wrote an admiring biography. The main facts about Dante's personal life that emerge from these sources, supplemented by sparse mentions in Florentine archives, are these: Dante was the son of a middle-ranking member of the Florentine merchant aristocracy, Alighiero, a notary and possibly a money-lender, who was heavily involved in the trading and banking world that Dante always pours scorn on. His mother died perhaps before he was 5 and his father soon remarried. In 1277 he was formally betrothed to Gemma Donati, from the powerful Donati family, and would marry her about eight years later. His wife's family would go on to play a prominent part in the events leading to his exile. He and Gemma had three sons, and a daughter, Antonia, who became a nun in Ravenna during Dante's residence there, taking the (to us) strikingly significant name of Beatrice. We may guess that Gemma followed her husband into exile, but we do not know for sure. Pietro, on the other hand, was almost certainly part of Dante's circle in Verona and Ravenna towards the end of his life, when Dante enjoyed a measure of security and was valued both as a scholar and as a poet. As far as Beatrice is concerned, we know next to nothing, but then early commentators were also at a loss. 'Who is this Beatrice?' asks Benvenuto da Imola in the 1370s. His only reply to the question is that she really was a beautiful Florentine lady. Boccaccio says she was Bice, daughter of a prominent Florentine named Folco Portinari, who in 1287 was married to Simone de' Bardi, from the wealthy banking family. Otherwise we are left with the Beatrice, meaning 'she who blesses' or 'confers beatitude', of Dante's works.

Florentine documents give us some hard information about Dante's political career. He was a prominent figure on the wrong side. He joined the guild of physicians and apothecaries in 1295 and thereby qualified to take on public office in the city. But the Guelf faction ruling Florence since the expulsion of the rival Ghibellines in the early 1270s were themselves divided. Of the two new groups that emerged, the Whites and the Blacks, the Whites initially had the upper hand, and Dante became a prominent White. His friend Cavalcanti was also a White, unlike his wife's family, the Donati. Dante held various positions and crucially was elected one of the six *Priori* (the senior executive body of the city) for the period June–August 1300. This was precisely the moment when Pope Boniface VIII arranged for the brother of the French king, Charles de Valois, to come to Tuscany and rid the city of the Whites. The result was a takeover in November 1301 by the Blacks, with Corso Donati at their head. Dante got away with his life because he was on a mission to the Pope in Rome at the time, but he and other prominent Whites were formally exiled in 1302. His property was confiscated, he was condemned to exile for barratry (corruption), and later placed under sentence of death if he should ever be found in Florentine territory. The exiled Whites joined up with the Ghibellines who were still hoping for a return, but their combined forces were politically and militarily ineffective. By 1304 Dante had broken with them, and became, as he puts it in *Paradiso* 17.69, a party for himself; all the same he actively promoted the invasion of Italy by the Emperor Henry VII, which he hoped would expel the Black Guelfs and restore the Pope to his proper spiritual role. When Henry died in 1313 and his expedition totally collapsed, Dante's prospects of a return to Florence did not completely disappear. The Florentines offered him a qualified and humiliating pardon in 1315. Understandably he turned it down, even if an almost desperate desire to return remained, and the death penalty was subsequently renewed.

Much of his exile remains obscure, especially the earlier years, before he established himself on a firm basis with the della Scala in Verona and then with Guido Novello da Polenta in Ravenna. In all probability he stayed in central and northern Italy, and stories of visits to southern France, or studies in Paris or even Oxford, are very likely fabrications. But he was undoubtedly well known, and by the end of his life the most famous poet of his time, no doubt primarily for the *Comedy*. The poem seems to have been started around 1307, and the first two parts at least seem to have been in circulation five or six years before his death. But he was also a respected Latin writer. He read out himself his *Quaestio de aqua et terra* to a distinguished audience in the Church of Sant'Elena in Verona; and he wrote two Latin *Eclogues* in reply to a prominent Bolognese scholar, Giovanni del Virgilio, who had written asking why he had written in the vernacular rather than Latin. He died in 1321 after falling ill during a mission to Venice for Guido Novello. Since some of his greatest admirers were Florentines, within a few decades Florence would be asking for the return of his body from its tomb in Ravenna. The request has never been granted, and the monumental 19th century tomb built for him in the Basilica of Santa Croce remains empty.

Vita nova and *Convivio*

Dante sees writing about oneself as a problem and, as with many other problems, he manages both to confront it head on and leave it open. As he says with approval in the sentence quoted at the head of this chapter, theorists of rhetoric, which for him embraced most literary composition, argue that no one should speak of themselves without just cause. In the same *Convivio* chapter (1.2) he argues that it is justified in two particular circumstances. The first is when the writer is defending himself against unjust or threatening attacks on his good name and his work; this he says is the case now that he is in exile, citing the precedent of Boethius, who wrote the *Consolation of Philosophy* in prison in the early 5th century AD. The second is when writing about oneself is a way of conveying something educational and beneficial to the reader, and here he cites St Augustine, whose review of his life in the *Confessions*, with its movement from sin and error through radical repentance to dedication to the Christian life, is usually read as paradigmatic for Christian readers. It has often been said that Dante has something similar in mind, to some extent in the *Vita nova* and even more in the *Comedy*, presenting himself at the start of the poem as an abject and ignorant sinner, who then gradually acquires intellectual, spiritual, and moral enlightenment. Certainly the objective facts of his life seem often to be selected, and also adjusted, to help bring similar enlightenment to others.

The *Vita nova* is Dante's first book and the only one apart from the *Comedy* which tells a story, arranging in chronological order the poems it brings together, and providing a narrative explanation of how they relate to each other, with commentaries on their structure and meaning. The story is an unusual and individual one, starting with the claim to have fallen overwhelmingly in love with Beatrice at the age of 9. From the beginning Dante stresses that it is a love that fully accords with the demands of reason (*ragione*), which means that it is not immoral or sensual, but potentially a source of moral and spiritual improvement. This is a view of love quite different from the questionable passions celebrated by most contemporary love literature, even though the idiom that Dante uses, and the attitudes represented in the early poems, have much in common with that kind of writing. His narrative up to the point of Beatrice's death is one of sometimes painful progress, as he learns to cease making demands of any sort on the loved person and to make his poetry solely one of praise and celebration. His *ragione* as poet and lover is put to an extreme test when Beatrice dies, her death causing the dramatic interruption of a poem of which Dante gives us the opening stanza. But a year after Beatrice's death, Dante finds his emotions stirring again for another woman who he thinks shows pity for him. He writes poems for this *donna pietosa* and tries to persuade himself that there is no conflict with his love for the dead Beatrice, yet the word that comes up repeatedly is *vile* ('base', 'abject', 'cowardly'), and his desire is an 'adversary of reason' (*VN* 40). Ultimately he redirects his emotions to Beatrice: the *Vita nova* ends with a vision of her in Heaven, and a resolution to write of her again at some later date when he has acquired the skills and means to do so. We cannot but think of the *Comedy*; in any event Beatrice has already triumphed to a degree achieved by no other woman a poet had claimed to love and written for, either before or probably since.

We may find the story incredible. It certainly has a very distinctive literary and poetic character. Dante meets people and has friends, familiar things happen such as illnesses, deaths, and departures, and the setting seems to be the real one of Florence, but all these things are merely sketched out in delicate musical prose. Periphrases take precedence over direct naming; key terms take on multiple connotations. Rather than the Italian *Vita nuova*, Dante's title is now thought to have been the Latin *Vita nova*, from the phrase 'Incipit vita nova' in the opening paragraph. In either form the title means 'new' or 'young life', but 'nova' also carries suggestions of 'extraordinary' or 'wondrous', both appropriate to a life and a life-story rich in spiritual and possibly miraculous significances. Beatrice is repeatedly associated with the number nine—a squaring of three and hence related to the Holy Trinity. Much of the narrative is carried forwards in an almost dreamlike way. In spite of the stress on reason, suggestion has the edge over explained meaning, especially in the prose. It is as if Dante is only up to a point able to make sense of his experiences, but is confident that the further senses that he does not and cannot grasp are there in and behind the evident enigmas. It is this interplay between the two poles of rational understanding and poetic or religious suggestion that gives the book its intriguing appeal and beauty.

Yet it is not really an allegory, or an exemplary story on the lines of Augustine's *Confessions*. Too much has to be left out if we try to see Dante as a typical Christian undergoing education in spiritual love, and a symbol of Theology or Christian Charity in the figure of Beatrice. At the same time the story is clearly a constructed one, with a deliberate focus, the power of which is evident even if its full significance has to remain implicit. Poems written earlier are given retrospective meanings that it is hard to feel the texts warrant. Others are said to be written for a 'screen' lady, to whom Dante pretends to be attached in order to deflect suspicions away from Beatrice. This might fit with the broadly courtly ethos, but it is hard not to feel that poems originally written for other women have been drafted into the *Vita nova* because they can play a part in the story of Dante's love for Beatrice. Vice versa Dante excludes some of his love poems of the period that are clearly written for other women, real or imagined, and other poems that present a much more idolatrous or even sensual image of his love for Beatrice.

We might also wonder how to place a group of poems of obsessive erotic desire written only a year or two later in a deliberately harsh style. These 'rime petrose' (*Rime* 43–6: 'stony rhymes') are quite out of kilter with Dante's thinking and practice in the *Vita nova*, and are often nowadays accounted for as stylistic experiments whose fruit will be evident in some of the poetry of the *Inferno* and even *Paradiso*. Dante himself valued the poems highly, and discusses the techniques they use in the *De vulgari eloquentia* (2.10 and 13), but neither there nor anywhere else does he try to fit them (or many other uncollected poems) into the history of his love for Beatrice and the poetry it is bound up with.

Further complications appear more than ten years later, when Dante looks back to Beatrice and the *Vita nova* in the *Convivio*. The earlier book, he says (*Conv.* 2.12), was a product of his youth, whereas the work he is now embarking on is more mature and rational. He is writing it not in order to deny or disparage the earlier work or the figure of Beatrice, but to reflect his commitment since her death to philosophy, from which he has derived great consolation for his loss, and the benefits of which he wishes to pass on to others. In spite of his protestations, ethics and issues of living happily and well in this world soon seem to displace the concern with transcendental matters. After various deeply respectful mentions of Beatrice, he declares quite early on (2.8) that he will not say anything further about her, and he keeps his word. Her displacement is then thrown into greater relief when Dante turns to the *donna pietosa* of the *Vita nova*, who had supplied consolation after Beatrice's death. He now says that this figure is a conscious fiction, a *donna gentile* (noble lady) who allegorically represents philosophy, and that his attraction to her in the earlier book stands for his philosophical interests. There is no mention of anything *vile* or irrational in his love for her, as there was in the *Vita nova*, and no reference to her rejection and the return to Beatrice at the end of the earlier book.

It is difficult to make sense of this transformation of the *donna pietosa* and the change of focus that goes with it. Some have posited that the *Vita nova* was rewritten at a later date, but there is no evidence at all that this ever happened. Nor is there any hint in the *Vita nova* that the *donna pietosa* is an allegorical figure, or, in the *Convivio*, that the allegorization might have repercussions on Beatrice's significance. Dante is clearly a selective recounter of his past, who casts different phases of his life and writing career in different lights according to his current aims. At the same time the remarkable fact remains that, unlike any medieval predecessors, he does have a serious autobiographical project. Whatever the gaps and inconsistencies, there is a conviction at work that the course of his life has an underlying sense which can be recounted, and can become meaningful to himself and to his readers.

The *Comedy*

The project is further developed in the *Comedy*, as are the perplexities we are likely to feel: what, we might ask, is Dante really saying about his personal history with this extraordinary narrative of a journey through the next life culminating in the vision of God?

The common assumption is that when Dante began writing the poem around 1307, some five years after his exile from Florence, he left the *De vulgari eloquentia* and *Convivio* unfinished in order to write it, though there are signs that both books had evolved as far as he was really interested in taking them. The journey itself is dated earlier, to when he was still living in Florence, but from the beginning the personal intersects with the general and the symbolic on a much grander scale than in anything he had written before. He is 35 years old, halfway through the life of man, near the age as Christ was held to be when he was crucified, and the day of the descent into Hell is Good Friday. The year 1300, in which the journey is set, was not only the start of a new century, but had been declared by Pope Boniface VIII as a Jubilee, in which pilgrims to Rome could gain additional remission of their sins. The full implications may not be immediately decodable, but they obviously make the journey much more than just an account of personal experience, though it is that too, and in very important ways.

The interaction between the personal and the general is given a crucially important formulation at the very start of the poem. Canti 1 and 2 of *Inferno* have an introductory function and are quite different from almost everything that follows. They place the journey through the afterlife in relation to Dante's own life on earth, through an abstract, unreal, dream-like narrative. Dante emerges from a dark wood in which he had been lost, and attempts to climb an unspecified sun-lit mountain. He is prevented from doing so by three animals, a lion, a leopard, and a wolf, the third of which begins to drive him back. He is rescued by the appearance of the poet Virgil, who has been sent by Dante's beloved Beatrice (instigated in turn by St Lucy acting on behalf of the Virgin Mary) to take him to the same goal by another route, through Hell and Purgatory; after that Beatrice herself will lead Dante to Paradise.

All of this only makes sense as allegory, and its meaning becomes clearer as Dante's journey through the afterlife progresses. The mountain is a first image of the mountain of Purgatory, with the Earthly Paradise on top, which in turn represents the moral perfection that humans should aspire to in this life. The dark wood is the state of sin into which Dante fell after Beatrice died, and which she reproaches him for when they are reunited in the Earthly Paradise. Virgil seems to be partly the Roman poet, partly the embodiment of human reason—a question we shall return to in the next chapter. The three beasts make most sense as standing for sins in the world more than in Dante, who has seemingly left sin behind in the dark wood: the lion is pride, the leopard lust, and the wolf avarice; the latter, the beast that turns Dante back, is repeatedly blamed later in the poem as the source of the world's corruption (e.g. *Purg.* 20.10–12). One major significance of Dante's journey, though as we shall see not the only one, thus seems to be that of personal moral salvation, resulting from a special act of divine grace, and made necessary by the world's current state.

The journey is cast as a return to Beatrice and the moral and spiritual inspiration she bestowed on him. In this respect the narrative of the *Vita nova* (though not that of the *Convivio*) feeds relatively easily into the *Comedy*, and Dante himself from time to time alludes to moments described in the earlier book. The most intensely personal moment in the entire poem comes when Beatrice appears before him in the Earthly Paradise, and when Virgil, who has been his guide and support until then, disappears. The symbolism is intense and multivalent, centring on a pageant representing the history of humanity and the Church. At the centre of this pageant is Beatrice, who herself takes on vast symbolic resonances and has been variously identified with Christ, the Church, and Theology. But what Dante chooses to do at the moment when she reveals herself to him is to dwell on the reawakening of his own desires, giving them at this moment an almost erotic colouring, and then, completely unexpectedly, have her berate him for his moral failings and for what sound like his

24

infidelities. Whatever Beatrice may symbolize, she is also at this point a very assertive, even jealous woman. Her opening address to Dante is startling, not least because for the first and only time in the *Comedy* he is here identified by name:

> Dante, perché Virgilio se ne vada,
> non pianger anco, non piangere ancora,
> ché pianger ti convien per altra spada.
> [Dante, though Virgil goes away,
> do not weep yet, do not weep yet,
> since you must weep for another sword [that will pierce you].]
>
> (*Purg.* 30.55–7)

Dante immediately apologizes to the reader: his own name, he says, is registered here only out of necessity (l. 63). While he does not spell out what the necessity is, there is here a fundamental refusal to allow his own individuality to be subsumed into the general or the allegorical; the same applies to Virgil and Beatrice, also emphatically referred to by name in this episode. Here, as elsewhere, Dante is implicitly asserting that the personal and universal somehow fit together.

Characteristically, Dante is here less than specific about the nature of the failings for which Beatrice reproaches him. While she had kept him on the right path during her life, she says, after her death he turned away from her, 'following false images of good' (30.131), which in Dante's ethics is simply the generic definition of sin. Appearing to him in dreams, as she did at the end of the *Vita nova*, was of no avail: he fell so low that the only way to save him was to send him on the journey through Hell. While this underlines the meaning of the dark wood of *Inferno* 1, as a state of aberration after the return to Beatrice at the end of the *Vita nova*, it does not itself tell us what Dante's sin was. But in the next canto Beatrice alludes to his being led astray at an age when he should have known better by a 'pargoletta | o altra novità con sì breve uso' (31.59–60: 'a young girl | or some other novelty of such brief use'). Since a *pargoletta* does appear in some pre-exile poems (*Rime*

34–6), and a later *canzone* apparently written in the Casentino represents erotic obsession with a young girl (*Rime* 53), sexual infidelity may indeed be the charge. Alternatively, or in addition, the *pargoletta* might be allegorical, standing for some kind of intellectual deviation. From the viewpoint of the *Comedy*, the *Convivio* itself could reflect a period of excessive worldly interests, though as we shall see there are substantial continuities between the treatise and the poem.

An earlier episode in Purgatory casts another light on the meaning of the dark wood and Beatrice's reproaches. In canto 23, among the souls purging themselves of the sin of gluttony, Dante meets his old friend Forese Donati, and expresses regret for the life that they had led together, from which, he says, Virgil saved him. We have some evidence of the nature of that life in a series of scabrous sonnets that the two of them exchanged (*Rime* 26–8), in which they trade oblique jocular insults about gluttony, poverty, thievery, sexual inadequacies, and failure to deal with family obligations. The exchange (assuming it is genuine) probably belongs to the early 1290s, when Dante was also writing the *Vita nova*, and therefore when, we might suppose, he should have been devoted to the memory of Beatrice. In style and content it has much in common with the early *Fiore*—if this is by Dante—with its frankly erotic summary of the story of the *Roman de la Rose*.

In the end we can only conjecture what the failings were from which Dante represents himself as returning to Beatrice and everything she stood for, and we must accept that major developments in the overall story cannot be clarified. Did Dante have in mind a series of lapses or a gradual process? And how far is the whole story simply a literary construct? In one way, at least, the element of construction is quite clear. Dante as the central character in the *Comedy* is very different from the strong authorial voice that tells the story and delivers violent diatribes against the contemporary world. The character is no hero, no man of action; he undertakes his journey because superior powers want him to, and is totally dependent on encouragement and support from his two guides. It is only as a result of his journey that Dante will become the strong, prophetic poet, who will shoulder his exile with pride and tell the world truths it needs to hear. Only then will he acquire the heroic stature celebrated by European Romantics and Risorgimento patriots.

Dante's is not as a private vision. Throughout the *Comedy* he emphasizes the exceptional character of his experiences, but this serves to validate important general truths. He has either lived through those truths, or else they have been imparted to him as an individual, and hence are not offered to the reader simply as abstractions. The abstract generalizing discourse so abundant in Dante has a dynamic evolving quality because it is almost always presented in relation to an individual who is himself in a constant dynamic evolution. Seen in this light his severe editing of his personal life and careful shaping of what is left has precisely the purpose of focusing the attention on what really counts in a spiritual sense.

Historically Dante breaks new ground in his use of autobiography, for all the puzzles he may create for modern readers. In the early 12th century Peter Abelard had charted his tragic experiences as a lover. Otherwise stories of individual lives during the Middle Ages are generally schematic biographies of saints or princes. No poet before Dante, in the Middle Ages or antiquity, had written an account of his growth as a lover and poet comparable to the *Vita nova*, let alone one that showed such complex self-awareness. None had even begun to articulate the relationship between two works as connected and as different as the *Vita nova* and the *Convivio*. And no other writer, not even Augustine in the *Confessions*, had projected himself in the way Dante does in the *Comedy*, as a exceptional exemplary figure, drawn out of moral and spiritual squalor to become the voice of righteousness and truth, while at the same time retaining his historical specificity as an individual. The forms that Dante's autobiographical writing takes are in many ways unique to him, but writing about oneself and one's life, trying to find a sense in it, or using it as a springboard for the exploration of other issues, will be one of the major currents in Renaissance literature—beginning in the next generation with Petrarch, who, in this regard as in many others, absorbs Dante's precedent and radically recasts it.

Chapter 3
Truth

> Aguzza qui, lettor, ben li occhi al vero,
>
> ché 'l velo è ora ben tanto sottile,
>
> certo che 'l trapassar dentro è leggero
>
> [Sharpen well your eyes here, reader, to the truth,
>
> for the veil is now indeed so fine,
>
> that it is surely easy to penetrate within it]
>
> (*Purg.* 8.19)

The journey of the *Comedy*

Dante's idea of the physical universe was substantially that of his time, following a tradition going back to Ptolemy's 2nd century *Almagest* and beyond. The earth was round and located at the centre of the cosmos, surrounded in the first place by seven spheres occupied by the visible 'planets', in order the Moon, Mercury, Venus, the Sun, Mars, Jupiter, and Saturn. Beyond them lay the sphere of the Fixed Stars, and then the *Primum Mobile*, or crystalline sphere, a later addition to Ptolemy's system, from which the movement of all the others was held to derive. The outermost sphere was also a later addition: surrounding everything else, but in reality beyond time and space, was the Empyrean, literally the heaven of fire, the Christian Heaven, the abode of God and the souls of the blessed. The globe of the earth was itself divided into a southern hemisphere of water, and a northern hemisphere partly occupied by the mass of dry land stretching from the equator to the Arctic Circle. Dante saw this as occupying exactly half of the hemisphere's circumference, with the straits of Gibraltar at its westernmost and the mouth of the Ganges at its easternmost ends, and Jerusalem at the very centre (see Figure 4).

Once past the allegorical opening, Dante's narrative distances itself for most of its course from earlier vision literature of the Middle Ages. From the moment when, guided by Virgil, Dante passes through the entrance to Hell in canto 3 of *Inferno*, the journey of the *Comedy* is clearly and precisely located in contemporary geography and cosmology. His Hell, Purgatory, and Paradise can be quite accurately mapped according to the beliefs of his time, and usually are in editions of the *Comedy*, as they are in Figure 4. Dante does not say where the entrance is, but he envisages Hell as an empty cone reaching down to the very centre of the globe, where Satan is confined after being cast down from Heaven by God. The mountain of Purgatory, with the Earthly Paradise at its summit, is an island located in the Southern hemisphere of water exactly opposite Jerusalem (*Purg.* 4.79–84). The location and origin, though not the conception, of both Purgatory and the Earthly Paradise seem to have been Dante's invention. Virgil explains (*Inf.* 34.118–26) that Satan's fall into the southern hemisphere caused the land there to flee to its present location in the north, and suggests that it probably also caused earth to flee southwards and throw up the mountain of Purgatory.

Like its geography and cosmology, the journey's chronology is also precise, though sometimes difficult to determine because of the figurative way in which the various time references are expressed, and because of the variations in dating practice in his time. The whole journey lasts just over a week. It begins with entry into Hell at nightfall on Good Friday 1300. Echoing the story of Christ's death and resurrection, Dante and Virgil emerge at the foot of Mount Purgatory on Easter Day at dawn. They spend three nights on the mountain, and Dante undergoes his final purification in

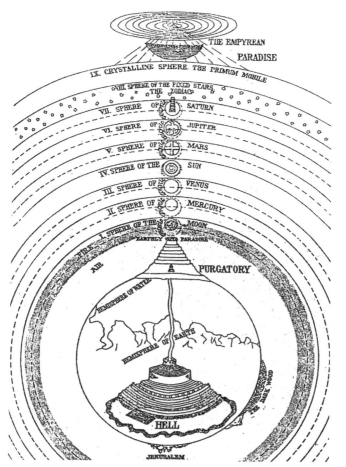

The following text labels appear within the figure:

THE EMPYREAN
PARADISE
IX. CRYSTALLINE SPHERE. THE PRIMUM MOBILE
VIII. SPHERE OF THE FIXED STARS
THE ZODIAC
VII. SPHERE OF SATURN
VI. SPHERE OF JUPITER
V. SPHERE OF MARS
IV. SPHERE OF THE SUN
III. SPHERE OF VENUS
II. SPHERE OF MERCURY
I. SPHERE OF THE MOON
EARTHLY PARADISE
FIRE
AIR
PURGATORY
HEMISPHERE OF WATER
HEMISPHERE OF EARTH
HELL
JERUSALEM

4. **General map of the Afterworld.** Adapted from Michelangelo Caetani, *La materia della Divina commedia di Dante Allighieri dichiarata in vi tavole* (Montecassino, c.1870).

the Earthly Paradise at mid-day. He then seems to ascend immediately into the Heavens where, in keeping with their nature, exact time references are no longer made.

Many other features of Dante's narrative contribute to this sense of a journey similar to one on earth. For all their supernatural mission, his two guides have notable human dimensions and an intense personal relationship with Dante the character. After her initial harshness in the Earthly Paradise, Beatrice is loving, beautiful, and by turns knowledgeable and fiercely polemical. Virgil is a paternal, inspiring figure, and also a tragic one, who is excluded from Paradise only because he lived before the coming of Christ, and for whom Dante weeps when he disappears. The appearance of the different circles into which Hell is divided, the souls of unrepentant sinners that the poets meet as they descend, the nature of the punishments, and the details of the sometimes hazardous descent, are all represented with distinctive visual realism, and, in the case of Brunetto, Ulysses, and other figures we shall come to later, with a dense human complexity. The massive three-headed figure of Satan, who protrudes towards our hemisphere from the earth's centre where he is permanently fixed in ice, is terrifyingly silent; but Dante describes precisely how he and Virgil climb down Satan's body, and then turn themselves round to head upwards past his feet along a tunnel away from the northern hemisphere. The shores of the mountain of Purgatory, onto which they emerge, and the Earthly Paradise, the biblical Garden of Eden which they reach at the top, are described in an idyllic language that evokes the beauties of nature on earth; and on their way up the mountain's seven terraces (Dante's term is *cornice*, 'ledge'), they encounter penitent souls as interesting in human terms as some of the damned, although their main concern is purification. When Dante rises up with Beatrice into Paradise, he is literally rising above the earth. Yet he is unremittingly eager for us to imagine the light displays which he says he saw, and the heavenly music he says he heard. The experience may contradict earthly expectations from the beginning, not just because of the flying, but because somehow Dante, a being with a physical body, enters other physical bodies, the planets. That Dante chooses to emphasize the paradox (*Par.* 2.31–42) only highlights the exceptional nature of what happens to him, not its unreality. And though the souls that he meets are hidden in light and their earthly selves are transformed, their appearance and movements are described with his usual precision. (See Boxes 3–5 for details of the divisions of Hell, Purgatory, and Paradise).

It would be a modern reader with a rare turn of mind, not to say a deranged one, who took Dante at face value and believed he made an actual journey through the afterlife, as if it were a journey from Florence to Bologna. Yet the narrative sometimes asks us to do just this. There are moments, particularly in Hell, when the truth claims are carried to surprising extremes; for instance, when Dante describes the frighteningly improbable monster Gerione, itself 'that foul image of deceit' (*Inf.* 17.7), swimming up through the dark air to carry him and Virgil down to the circle of fraud, he swears to the reader that he actually saw it (16.127–32). This and other such statements are rhetorical devices, of course, but they are more than mere conventions, and they are certainly not deployed ironically; in one sense or another, Dante wants us to believe him.

Theories of allegory

Boccaccio tells a story of Dante's amusement at overhearing a group of Veronese women who put his tanned face and curly beard down to singeing during visits to Hell. Early commentators were less naive, and generally focused on the ways in which the poem conveys truth or truths to the reader allegorically, not through literal representation. Dante's son, Pietro Alighieri, begins his commentary on his father's work by pointing out that it is figurative. The truths which it contains are hidden, he says, in language which is itself not to be taken literally. Others went further, keen to defend Dante against accusations of impiety. Of course, they said, the sinners are not really where Dante put them, most notably the popes whom Dante named and shamed in *Inferno* 19 for simony, selling church benefits for profit: they and all the other figures in the poem are moral examples. Approaches like this fit with the exhortation to the reader at the head of this chapter, to pass beyond the veil of the narrative to the truth that lies beneath; there is another similar exhortation in *Inferno* 9.61–3. But Dante's main discussions of allegory—both short, though they have generated an immense amount of discussion—come elsewhere.

After a brief excursus on the personification of Love in the *Vita nova*, the subject is addressed in more detail at the beginning of Book 2 of the *Convivio*. Theologians had written for centuries about the four senses of biblical texts: literal, allegorical, moral, and anagogical or spiritual—the last term derives from the Greek *anagoge*, a 'leading up', and refers to meanings relating to the next life. Alongside this there was an established practice of poetic interpretation, mostly applied to classical works, which usually distinguished simply between the literal and allegorical senses. Apart from the number of levels, the fundamental difference between the two approaches was that in biblical interpretation the literal level, as God's word, was taken to be true; in poetry, on the other hand, it was generally taken to be false: Christians could not accept as literally true the pagan mythology that so much classical poetry is about. Somewhat confusingly, Dante's schema in the *Convivio* conflates the two approaches: he lists the four senses of biblical exegesis, but defines and illustrates the literal and allegorical meanings from classical poetry, and the moral and anagogical from the Bible. Poetry's literal sense is a 'fable', the allegorical sense hidden under it is the 'truth concealed beneath a beautiful lie'. Dante's example is the myth in Ovid's *Metamorphoses* of Orpheus calming the beasts and making the mountains move with the music of his lyre; this allegorically signifies the moral truth that the wise man uses language to civilize and educate the brutish.

Dante notes that theologians understand the allegorical sense differently, a point to which we shall return shortly. Here in the *Convivio* he is mainly concerned with poetic allegory as it was commonly understood in the Middle Ages. In medieval poetic practice this usually took the form of the personification of abstract ideas or prosopopoeia, as in the *Roman de la Rose*, or later in *Pilgrim's Progress*. In the interpretation of poetry abstract and general meanings were also attributed to apparently concrete and individual figures, as in Dante's Orpheus example. Dante's personification of Love in the *Vita nova* is an example of the former; the claim that the *donna pietosa* of the *Vita nova* is an allegory of philosophy is an example of the latter. The latter kind of allegory also dominates the first two canti of *Inferno*, as we have seen. But with its highly concrete, specific, and personal character and its apparent claims to literal truth, the rest of the *Comedy* is much more difficult to read in such a way. Although it has all sorts of further dimensions of meaning, in this respect it is a very different work from the *Roman de la Rose* or *Pilgrim's Progress*.

In fact there are strong indications that, by the time he wrote the *Comedy*, Dante's thinking had moved on beyond the idea of poetic allegory. Some of these appear in the poem itself. But there is also a long Latin letter (*Ep.* 13), which dedicates the *Paradiso* to Dante's patron Can Grande della Scala, the ruler of Verona, and explains in very general terms what it and the *Comedy* as a whole are about. There have been heated arguments about the letter's authenticity, but there is much in it that is recognizably Dantesque, or at the very least must derive ultimately from Dante, even if the letter might not have been written directly by him. We shall follow the prevailing view and treat it as genuine, though it offers no easy solutions to the question of the *Comedy*'s real meaning.

The letter returns to the four levels of biblical exegesis, asserting that the *Comedy* is *polysemos*, i.e. has many senses, and explaining how this works by reference to the opening of Psalm 113, which speaks literally of Israel coming out of the land of Egypt. The

allegorical sense is 'our redemption wrought by Christ', the moral
sense 'the conversion of the soul from the grief and misery of sin
to the state of grace', and the anagogical sense 'the departure of
the holy soul from the slavery of this corruption to the liberty of
eternal glory'. There is no mixture here of the biblical and the
poetic, as there was in the *Convivio*: the literal meaning is
historically true, not fictitious, and the allegorical sense is not a
moral proposition, as in the example of Orpheus, but another
supposedly real event. In this respect Dante is following the
long-established belief that events in the Old Testament are an
allegory in the sense of a *figura* or prefiguration of those in the
New: the Old Testament's narrative of the exodus of Israel
prefigures the New Testament's narrative of the Redemption. The
implication is a highly unusual, even a preposterous one for a
medieval writer. Dante seems to be suggesting that the method of
biblical interpretation is applicable to his own poetic work.

Is Dante really claiming something like biblical status for the
Comedy? This would certainly fit with the poem's apparent
claims to literal truth, but it is as hard for us as for the early
commentators to accept these claims at face value, to see the poem
as true in the way that, for many at least, the Bible is true. Some
critics have argued that Dante only wanted us to read the *Comedy*
as if the literal sense were true, to suspend our knowledge that it
is not in order to lend force to his vision, but that might quickly
take us back to some version of poetic allegory. The problems do
not stop there. It is hard in practice to apply the fourfold scheme
of meanings systematically to the *Comedy*, as many early
commentators and some later ones tried to do with very mixed
success. We can see up to a point how it might work in the most
general terms: the upward nature of the journey is anagogical, and
we can pull out moral senses easily enough. On the other hand
there is something forced about any attempt to find in the *Comedy*
equivalents of the Old Testament's prefigurations of the New, of
the kind that medieval commentators found in the Bible. It is
telling that, once he has run through the fourfold scheme in the

letter, Dante does not make any further use of it to interpret his own work, and collapses the three non-literal meanings into a single wide-ranging allegorical sense.

In any case the opposition between poetic and theological allegory was always an oversimplification. Nobody in Dante's time, for instance, could take the love poetry of the biblical Song of Songs as anything but a fictional allegory of the Church's love for God. Vice versa, Lucan's epic poem on the Roman Civil War, *De bello civili*, was considered historically true, and up to a point so too was Virgil's *Aeneid*. Even more than these ancient texts, Dante's poem confounds the distinction between the two types of allegory, for in the end neither poetic nor theological allegory gives us an adequate way to handle its full richness and complexity. Dante's implicit equation of the *Comedy* with the Bible may just have been a way of recognizing and asserting that it is uncategorizable within the terms he and his contemporaries had available.

Allegory in the *Comedy*

According to the letter to Can Grande, the literal subject of the poem is 'the state of souls after death', the allegorical sense is 'man, as by good or ill deserts, in the exercise of the freedom of his will, he becomes liable to rewarding or punishing justice'. It is a broad, somewhat enigmatic formulation, in which the proposed allegorical meaning seems to do little more than articulate in terms of human action on earth what we might think is anyway implied in the literal sense. But what Dante says here connects with, and may be intended to reflect, an issue developed at length in his late political treatise, the *Monarchia*.

Concluding the main argument of its third and final book, Dante declares (3.16) that divine providence has established two ends for humanity: happiness on earth and happiness in Heaven. The former is figured ('figuratur') by the Earthly Paradise, the latter is signified ('intelligi datur') by the Heavenly Paradise, and providence has determined that mankind should be led to the former under the guidance of reason, philosophy, and the Holy Roman Emperor, and to the latter under that of the theological virtues of faith, hope, and charity, scripture, and the Pope. The distinction is fundamental to Dante's political thinking, and we shall return to it in Chapters 5 and 6. It also points to a general allegorical or figurative meaning of the main plot of the *Comedy*, most of which had probably been completed by the time the *Monarchia* was written, and offers the strongest evidence we have of the allegorical meaning its author intended. Virgil guiding Dante to the Earthly Paradise stands for the Emperor guiding mankind to earthly happiness through reason and philosophy, Beatrice guiding Dante to Heaven proper stands for the Pope guiding mankind to heavenly happiness through the theological virtues and scripture.

Generalizing the allegory still further, so as not to limit it to Dante's views on politics, we can see Dante the pilgrim as the morally and spiritually lost individual who is morally purified through reason, and then achieves spiritual salvation through faith, hope, and charity. Some of the details of Dante's narrative can be used to make the allegory more complex. Reason (Virgil) is itself stimulated into action by the action of divine grace, described in *Inferno* 2 as passing from the Virgin to St Lucy, then to Beatrice, and finally to Virgil. By itself it can acquaint the soul primarily with moral negatives (Hell) and even then may need the divine help which is given at crucial moments in the course of the poets' journey. Once the soul has taken the negatives on board and is ready for more positive lessons, divine help becomes more necessary, as is evident throughout Dante's ascent in Purgatory. Eventually a stage is reached when the soul has made sufficient progress to be able to receive divine enlightenment and love more directly. Grace and knowledge of the divine or theology (Beatrice) educate the soul in matters which reason cannot reach to by itself (hence Virgil's disappearance), though that does not mean that there is not a rational component in what divine wisdom has to say. The highest form of enlightenment is however beyond human language and thought, even of the most exalted kind. Beatrice herself gives way to the mystic St Bernard, who leads Dante to his final vision, the nature of which can only be sketched out rather than analysed or described.

This interpretation has its difficulties, as we shall see in the next chapter, nor would every critic or scholar put the allegory in quite this way. Most would agree, however, that the poem is concerned to press upon us some message or messages of moral or spiritual progress. In any event this sort of allegorical interpretation of Dante's progress seems to work best only in the sort of general terms we have just used. If Dante is very broadly speaking an Everyman, he is still also a highly specific individual. Nor is there any step-by-step process of education as he journeys through the three realms. Progress is rather through accumulation, diversity, and digression. As Dante constantly repeats, his journey is a privilege granted to him alone, and it follows a route quite different from that which should be available to mankind as a whole but currently is not. Allegory as normally understood, and as Dante formulates it, always turns on similarities between image and underlying sense. In the *Comedy* it is again and again the differences or even discrepancies between the two that stand out.

If interpreted as stating that a clear and consistent hidden sense runs through the whole poem, therefore, the veil image at the head of this chapter is misleading, and leaves too much out of account. Rather than searching for a single hidden meaning or set of meanings just below the surface, we will do better to look for levels of sense that are multiple, at times overwhelmingly so. Meanings collide, merge, and at times contradict each other, and are developed in novel and startling ways that become more intensely inventive as the poem progresses. The mode of writing keeps shifting according to imaginative and intellectual requirements that branch out in far more directions than can be embraced in a single formula; the ways to the truth or truths that

Dante wants us to grasp are rarely straightforward, while the truths themselves are more open-ended than we might expect. 'Messo t'ho innanzi: omai per te ti ciba' (*Par.* 10.25: 'I've set [the dish] before you. Now feed yourself on your own account'), he urges the reader after a brief but none too easy exposition of the movement of the zodiac, and he will intimate elsewhere too that reader participation is essential for understanding. That does not mean, of course, that there is no authorial aid or direction.

Let us look at two episodes to see how different modes of writing and different dimensions of meaning intersect and interact. The first is one of the most famous in the whole poem: the meeting with Francesca da Rimini in the circle of the lustful in *Inferno* 5. This is where Dante encounters for the first time souls who have not repented, and the way the episode proceeds is a blueprint for the many others that follow. These souls are 'i peccator carnali | che la ragion sommettono al talento' (*Inf.* 5.38-9: 'the carnal sinners who subject reason to desire'). Their punishment is to be swept along by a violent, unrelenting gale, which takes them up and down in the infernal darkness in constantly changing directions. We can quite easily agree with early commentators that this is an image, or an allegory, of the blind force of lust or passion. But once Dante singles out individual named souls in what will become his characteristic way, then this sort of allegory fades into the background.

The two lovers Paolo and Francesca are allowed to stop for a few moments to speak with Dante. Francesca, the wife of the ruler of Rimini, recounts her love for her brother-in-law Paolo and their murder by her husband not many years before the date of Dante's journey. As she does so a great deal more comes into play regarding the behaviour of the lovers as individuals and the implications of her narrative. Rather than a story of simple lust, it is one of adulterous erotic passion, and is articulated in the terms of contemporary love poetry and romance. The two lovers are compared to a pair of doves as they fly towards Dante and Virgil, and enjoy the remarkable privilege of remaining together even in their eternal punishment. Francesca speaks to Dante with elegant, engaging courtesy, and there is intense pathos in her account of the beginning of her affair. All this raises questions as to what distinguishes this love from Dante's love for Beatrice, the virtuous nature of which he claims to have no doubts about whatsoever. Many readers, particularly in the 19th century, have been left with the impression that Francesca is a victim with whom we and Dante himself cannot help but sympathize. Modern critics tend to stress her culpability and to treat Dante's sympathy for her, which eventually leads to his fainting, as the painful recognition of just how close to damnation he might have come. Whichever way we see Francesca, there is no convincing way of allegorizing her completely. It is noticeable that Boccaccio's commentary, which goes on at length about lust in general, gives us the historical background, but has nothing to say about Francesca as allegory, or about the general implications of her speech.

On the other hand the lines at the head of this chapter do point to an obviously allegorical component in the canto in which they occur (*Purg.* 8). Dante and Virgil are finishing the first day's climb up Mount Purgatory and have just met the poet Sordello. He escorts them to a shallow dip in the mountain side where they are to pass the night; progress up the mountain has always to stop when darkness falls, meaning allegorically, when divine grace (the light of the sun) is temporarily removed. However there is still divine protection in the form of two angels with green wings, dressed in green robes. When a preening serpent slinks in, the angels swoop down and chase it off: hope, represented by the colour green, thus repels the seductions of the world and keeps the Christian soul safe until grace is once again bestowed. So far the meaning seems straightforward; we can decode a clear moral and spiritual message that we can be pretty sure Dante wants to impress on us. But how does this relate to two encounters that are intercalated between the appearance of the angels and the chasing off of the serpent?

The first is with an old friend of Dante's whom he greets with delight: 'Noble Judge Nino, how pleased I was | when I saw you were not among the wicked' (8.53–4). Nino Visconti speaks of the self-seeking marriages his widow has contracted since his death, and his concern that his virtuous daughter Giovanna should pray for him. Do these examples of woman's inconstancy and virtue respectively connect with the seductive serpent that the angels chase away? Perhaps. What we can be sure of is that neither Nino nor his wife and daughter are allegorical figures in the way the angels and the serpent are; they are individual and historical, though also examples we can learn from. The second encounter is even less generalizable: it is with Currado Malaspina, whose family Dante praises, and who tells Dante in reply that he will soon experience their generosity at first hand. This episode in turn loops back to the issue of princely corruption and its rare exceptions, which had been discussed at some length in the previous canto and is now taken up in an autobiographical vein. All things considered, the injunction in *Purgatorio* 8 to penetrate the veil, like the similar one in *Inferno* (9.61–3), makes most sense as alerting the reader to the specific and limited instance of allegory in the episode, and at the same time pointing to the need to keep on interpreting, even if in other places the veil is too thick to lend itself even to the partial decoding that we can carry through here.

Up to a point the veil lifts as the poem progresses. *Inferno* is dramatic, striking, varied, concrete, in many ways immediately graspable, with barely any of the doctrinal, scientific and philosophical discourses that will appear later. But Dante's, and the reader's, understanding of what is going on is very limited in rational or intellectual terms, as is appropriate to the realm of evil and materiality. In Purgatory rational understanding becomes more possible, through explicit expositions and through allegory. But it still remains incomplete, both for the souls and even more so for Dante, who retains an earthly body and perceptions. Limitations are stressed even more in *Paradiso*. When Dante is told in the Heaven of the Moon that the souls he sees really reside in the highest heaven of all, and only appear to him in the lower heavens for his benefit, he is highlighting his own and his readers' incapacity to understand ultimate truth. *Paradiso* is a demonstration that metaphor or allegory are inevitable; direct apprehension of divine reality means going beyond human language and comprehension. Seen in this light, Dante's journey is also a journey through language, in particular through the possibilities given to poetry to articulate and understand its own truth and the truth, or truths, to which it refers.

In the end, given the complexities of his project, it should not surprise us that Dante has to struggle with the interpretation of his own work. The *Comedy* is truly 'polysemous' in the sense that its meanings cannot be fully controlled or systematized. Too many scholars have searched for a clear and consistent system of ideas behind the poem, and in doing so have tended to ignore much of its richness and power. Our own reading embraces without apology a central tenet of modern critical thinking, that the meaning of poetry exceeds the capacity of conceptual language to explain it, particularly the language of the time in which it is written, and all the more so in the case of a writer as bold and original as Dante. Ideas and their relationship with each other are plainly of immense importance in almost everything he wrote, and we shall look at various aspects of his thinking in the chapters that follow. But, as some early commentators were quick to note, he is primarily a poet, not a philosopher. As a poet, he sets ideas and problems in imaginative relations with each other when intellectual analysis and synthesis fail, which means creating dynamic tensions and ambiguities as well as moments of resolution. The constant assertion of the literal truth of his journey, implausible even by the standards of his own time, is one of the ways in which he does this: it challenges the reader both to interpret freely, and to recognize and think about the inevitable limits of any interpretation.

Chapter 4
Writing

> I' mi son un che, quando
> Amor mi spira, noto, e a quel modo
> ch'e' ditta dentro vo significando
> [I am one who when
> Love breathes in me, takes note and registers
> according to the way that he dictates within]
>
> (*Purg.* 24.52–4)

Latin and Italian

Like many others of his time, Dante was a bilingual writer. The greater part of his work is in Italian, the language he and others called the *volgare* or vernacular. He also wrote prose and some verse in Latin. His only foray into another language that we know of for sure is the moving speech in Provençal that he assigns to the troubadour, Arnaut Daniel, in *Purgatorio* 26. He had at least a reading knowledge of French, perhaps a good one, but so far as we know he chose not to follow the example of Brunetto Latini and other Italians and write in the language. It was, he declares, a language best suited to prose, in particular to romances, a genre he never seems to have wanted to try. He had picked up a few Greek scientific and philosophical terms from his Latin reading, but otherwise Greek was closed to him, as were all other languages.

44

As the normal language of the Church, the universities, public administration, and serious learning in general, Latin had much of the range and vitality of a living language. For Dante's contemporaries, writing in Latin was generally easier than writing in Italian, though to do it well with any ambition required skill and training, including knowledge of a whole range of literary, philosophical, and religious texts. Perhaps even before his exile, Dante had read his way into Virgil and other Latin poets, Cicero, Aristotle (in Latin translation), and other ancient thinkers. He also knew the Bible in the Vulgate version, and a range of authors from the fall of Rome through to Thomas Aquinas.

Dante writes in Latin when he has a cultured or prestigious readership in mind, and almost always with great rhetorical panache and with a good deal of his learning on view. All his thirteen surviving letters are in Latin, and most are addressed to persons of high rank. The *Monarchia* similarly takes on the Church's intelligentsia to argue in Latin that the Holy Roman Empire is independent of papal authority. Almost inevitably Latin is the medium of his most scholastic and, by the lights of the time, most scientific work, the *Quaestio de aqua et terra*. More surprisingly at first sight, Dante uses Latin in the *De vulgari eloquentia* (literally 'On vernacular eloquence'), one of the main arguments of which is that that the vernacular is the nobler of the two languages. The implicit purpose is to carry his case to a less provincial and more demanding readership than would be possible if the book were written in the vernacular itself.

There was no standard Italian as such in Dante's time, as we might expect in a country which had not been united politically since the fall of the Roman Empire. The spoken vernacular varied from region to region, even from city to city. The written vernacular was used for limited purposes and was generally dialectal, although some standardization had evolved. The one genre that constituted a tradition in the sense of an established set of writing practices was lyric poetry, which had come into being in Sicily around the second or third decade of the 13th century, and had been enthusiastically taken up in Tuscany a few decades later by the generation immediately preceding Dante's. There its range had expanded beyond the central theme of love to cover religious and moral topics as well as more down to earth or comic material. Otherwise there are scattered individual works or local traditions—religious poetry in Umbria and Lombardy, the odd chronicle, some sermons, some adaptations of Latin texts, some short stories (*novelle*), some letters with literary aspirations; romances and narrative poems will only appear after Dante's death. In many ways other Romance languages had more prestige. Northern Italians, such as Sordello (who Dante meets in *Purgatorio* 6), wrote their poetry in Provençal; as we have seen, Brunetto Latini tried popularizing learned material in French.

When Dante first tries his hand at writing in his late teens, he produces conventional love poetry. Thereafter he breaks new ground with every one of his works; even had he never written the *Comedy*, he would still have been the major writer in Italian of his time. Looking at his so-called minor works as a whole, we see running through them a constant effort to raise writing in Italian to the level of Latin, demonstrating that it can handle the same sort of complex themes with the same aesthetic assurance. We think of Dante primarily as a poet, as he did himself, but in the *Vita nova* and even more in the *Convivio* he creates the first prose in Italian to combine balance, order, musicality, and intellectual depth, integrating Latinate abstractions with the natural textures of Florentine, ridding the latter of its obviously local features—as well as, it must be said, of the sort of concreteness which English has always tended to favour.

Both the *Vita nova* and the *Convivio* purport to elucidate poems Dante had written earlier. At each stage self-commentary seems the precondition of another move forwards: setting previous practice in narrative and intellectual order and reaching appropriate theoretical conclusions leads to new writing which dynamically absorbs and goes beyond what has been achieved so far. It is a process which arguably only comes to an end in the last lines of *Paradiso*. Writing in a still inchoate literary vernacular left space for this kind of creativity; it also had to be defended. Dante first makes a serious case for the vernacular in the *Convivio*, stating that he wants to make the benefits of his philosophical studies available to others who do not have a knowledge of Latin, and are mostly taken up with the business of living. It is an anti-elitist educational stance that is itself a novel one for a medieval writer with intellectual ambitions, and which will underpin the far more complex project of the *Comedy*.

Before that comes the *De vulgari eloquentia*, which, in spite of being unfinished, marks a point of arrival in Dante's theorizing about the nature and status of the vernacular as a literary language vis-à-vis Latin, if not as regards his writing practice. To modern eyes, writing in Italian would seem natural, and writing in Latin artificial, and Dante was exceptional for his time in coming to see the issue in something like these terms. Following the view that prevailed until the mid-15th century, he believed that throughout its history Latin had existed side by side with the Italian and other vernaculars, not that the vernaculars developed out of it. The vernacular, he argues, is and always had been the mother tongue, learnt naturally from one's mother in infancy, and therefore having the qualities and the nobility of God's creation, nature itself. Latin is an artificial language, a *gramatica* created by men to counter the changes constantly taking place in the various vernacular languages, and able to reach out beyond the narrow geographical limits of any one of them. That gives it certain advantages, just as the great works written in Latin are in no way to be denigrated, and may well serve as models for vernacular writers. But the central conviction remains: 'nobilior est vulgaris' (1.2.1: 'the vernacular is the nobler'). It is this conviction that underpins the *Comedy* and that the *Comedy* aims to vindicate.

The *dolce stil novo*

The conviction that vernacular poetry has value and importance is clear from the *Vita nova* onwards. Chapter 25 argues that its subject par excellence is love, reflecting the reality that love poetry was the genre in which vernacular writing was most advanced. What is spectacular and unprecedented is Dante's claim in this chapter that vernacular love poetry has the same status and rights as poetry in Latin. The claim is backed up by the poems that Dante includes in the surrounding chapters, following on from the *canzone* 'Donne ch'avete intelletto d'amore' ('Ladies who have understanding of love'), which marked the decisive move to a poetry about Beatrice consisting solely in praise (see Figure 5). Contemporaries seem to have been impressed. 'Donne ch'avete' was known as far away as Bologna even before the *Vita nova* was completed. In *Purgatorio* 24 a poet of the previous generation, Bonagiunta da Lucca, asks Dante in amazement if he is the one who produced the new verse (*nove rime*) that begins with its opening line. Dante replies with the compressed and in some ways enigmatic lines quoted at the head of this chapter. For a poet to claim to follow the dictates of love may seem almost trite, but the lines are important both for Dante's earlier poetry and for the *Comedy* itself, and have powerful polemical resonances.

The Italian poets who first took up the work of the Sicilians were surprisingly mixed and wide-ranging. Notaries, merchants, bankers, and others joined in a kind of verse free-for-all, writing on love, moral issues, politics, and other subjects, sometimes with great verve and an almost experimental freedom of style. Few of them are mentioned in Dante's works. Such writers were simply not up to the standards which he and his friends set for poetry in the vernacular. The critical disdain becomes explicit in Dante's comments on Guittone d'Arezzo, the most famous and respected writer of Italian verse of the previous generation with

5. Dante Gabriel Rossetti, Beatrice Meeting Dante at a Wedding Feast. Pre-Raphaelite artists were particularly drawn to the Beatrice of the *Vita nova*.

a large and varied body of work to his name. Much of it anticipates Dante himself, as does Guittone's experience of (temporary) exile, and the related poems expressing his conviction of the rightness of his position and his aching desire to return to his native Arezzo. Some of Dante's early poems have a touch of Guittone's manner, but by the time he discovers his own voice he has no hesitations: Guittone is dismissed as a plebeian writer who never aspired to the noblest kind of poetry. When Bonagiunta hears Dante's statement about poetic inspiration in *Purgatorio*, he effectively admits his own poetic failure and that of Guittone and their predecessor Giacomo da Lentini, the writer usually credited with inventing the sonnet and the leading figure in the Sicilian School. All of them, says Bonagiunta, have fallen short of the 'dolce stil novo' (*Purg.* 24.57) that Dante has now explained to him.

The phrase, which appears here for the first time, means literally 'sweet new style', though *dolce* in old Italian is a much more forceful word than 'sweet' and lacks any cloying or sugary associations. As we said in Chapter 2, it is commonly used now as a label for a group of mostly Florentine poets writing in the 1290s. Its full meaning is not easy to pin down. In *Purgatorio* it suggests that for Dante the new poetry exemplified by 'Donne che avete' expressed a new depth of inspiration and discovered a new way of writing appropriate to it, encapsulated in the poetry of praise at the centre of the *Vita nova*. But none of the rest of the group developed anything like Dante's transcendental vision of love and the beloved; in all probability Cavalcanti broke with him precisely because he found that vision unacceptable. There was more agreement on the related point that Dante argued in the *Vita nova*, and later at greater length in the *Convivio*, that nobility (*gentilezza*) was a spiritual and moral quality, not a question of birth. Dante himself credited the argument to Guido Guinizelli, a Bolognese poet writing in the 1270s whom he addresses, when he meets him in *Purgatorio* (26.97–9), as his poetic father and father of all those who had written 'rime dolci e leggiadre' ('sweet attractive rhymes'). Quite a lot of *stilnovo* verse chimed with Guinizelli's idea of nobility, though it did not become the article of faith it is sometimes said to have been. As Dante himself seems to have viewed the matter, the real novelty and unifying factor in the *stil novo* group was the shared way of writing: the refined and deliberately restricted linguistic palette and the elevated mode of composition which, in the *De vulgari eloquentia*, he ascribes to the example of the major Latin poets, and finds in his own verse and that of his friends.

De vulgari eloquentia

By the time he wrote the *Convivio* and the *De vulgari eloquentia*, Dante no longer thought of himself primarily as a poet of love in the usual sense, but as a moral poet. His poems were not just beautiful; they were the result of feeding on the 'bread of the angels' (*Conv.* 1.2.1) at the banquet (hence the title *Convivio*) of wisdom and knowledge. This leads him in the *Convivio*'s second and third books to commentaries on two of his *canzoni* which re-interpret the poems' apparent love-content as representing philosophy. The moral project is carried through more fully in the last book, the longest of the four completed, which takes up the issue of nobility raised rather allusively in the *Vita nova*. The *canzone* on which it comments delivers an explicit rational discourse on this subject, which the commentary expands on. Dante had originally projected fifteen books and some of the other *canzoni* were already written; all of them, like the poem in *Convivio* 4, are deliberately challenging and in many ways deliberately unpoetic, perhaps almost Guittonian in comparison to his *stilnovo* poetry. It seems that love as a subject has now fallen into the background, as Beatrice herself had done. In the *De vulgari eloquentia* Dante will declare his younger friend Cino da Pistoia to be the principal Italian love poet, whilst he himself is the principal moral poet. It is a position he does not sustain in the *Comedy*, which will weave moral issues and love into its new and much more complex tapestry.

The *De vulgari eloquentia*'s opening assertion of the superiority of the vernacular over Latin leads into a broad discussion of the language, style, and subject matter appropriate to the best vernacular verse. The highest subjects are arms, love, and ethics, the established topics of serious poetry, and these high subjects require a correspondingly high language and style. The first of the treatise's two books conducts an unprecedented survey (still a major source for modern scholars) of the languages or dialects of the different parts of Italy, to determine which constitutes the 'illustrious vernacular' suited to such subjects. This is the first serious attempt to articulate the idea of a national vernacular language, but Dante's conclusion is that it is not spoken in any one part of the country. It is rather the language that underlies all regional usages and is to be found in the work of the best writers. Rather than some kind of standard Italian, it is a refined and elevated medium from which conspicuously local elements have been eliminated, and which is common to writers from different parts of the country—though in fact the writers he cites with approval are himself and other *stilnovo* poets. Ultimately it is not so much a language as a style.

The second of the treatise's two books is explicitly concerned with poetic composition, and generally reflects and retrospectively theorizes Dante's own practice in his lyric poetry. Previous vernacular poets had not theorized in any comparable way, though they clearly had a strong sense of stylistic hierarchy. On the one hand was the abstracted idiom of elevated love poetry, usually called courtly poetry, whether written at courts or not; on the other there was the more colloquial or idiomatic style that was used for parodying the former and for more earthy subjects. Dante had forayed into this *poesia giocosa* ('playful poetry'), as it is usually called in modern Italian, in his sonnet exchange with Forese Donati as well as in the *Fiore*, if he was its author. But all his important poems before the *Comedy* are in the much more elevated courtly style, even when he writes about sensual desire.

Dante now brings into play the widely accepted notion, going back to later classical times, that there are three levels of style, high, middle, and low, and that an author should choose between them according to the level of his subject matter. He terms the three styles tragic, comic, and elegiac, none of which adjectives are meant to refer to tragedy, comedy, or elegy in their normal senses, though his distinction between tragic and comic loosely reflects the stylistic differences between classical tragedy and comedy. His declared intention was to discuss in depth the constituents of all three styles over the four books of the treatise, but he broke off part of the way through Book 2, so that only the tragic style is dealt with extensively. This requires the highest subjects, and matches them with the highest verse forms, the highest constructions, and the highest vocabulary. The preferred metre should be the hendecasyllable, the eleven-syllable line that was already the established medium for serious vernacular poetry (and is the nearest Italian equivalent to the English iambic pentameter: see Box 2). The best verse form is the *canzone*, which interspersed hendecasyllables with seven-syllable lines, but in its highest realizations (for example in 'Donne ch'avete') used only the former.

Box 2 Dante's hendecasyllable

Italian versification is mainly syllable-based, not stress-based as in English and German: there is no fixed division into accented feet. The hendecasyllable is by definition a line in which the final accent falls on the tenth syllable. It usually has eleven syllables (hence the name), because in most Italian words the accent is on the penultimate, like *vita* in the first line of the *Comedy*:

Nel/mez/zo/del/cam/min/di/no/stra/vi/ta

But, if there are two syllables after the final accent (*márgini*), or if the last word ends with an accented syllable (*così*), a line will have respectively twelve syllables or only ten, as in:

O/ra/cen/por/ta/l' un/de'/du/ri/mar/gi/ni; (*Inf.* 15.1)
fuor/vi/vi, e/pe/rò/son/fes/si/co/sì. (*Inf.* 28.36)

There are a small number of lines of these last two types in the *Comedy*.

In Italian versification the general rule for counting syllables (marked by the forward slashes in the lines above) is that any sequence of one or more vowels, whether within or across word-boundaries, is considered to belong to a single syllable: thus '/vi/vi, e' in the line above has two syllables, not three as in normal parlance. However there are a large number of exceptions to this rule in the *Comedy*, far more than in later verse, and they are often quite random. Almost all lines in the *Comedy* have an accent on the fourth and/or sixth syllables, usually though not always followed by the phrase-break which became the norm in later verse.

From the examples Dante gives, it is clear that the constructions he has in mind involve complex syntax and extensive use of rhetorical figures, after the manner of the great classical authors and as prescribed in medieval rhetorical treatises. The vocabulary is highly selective, and takes due account of sound and cadence as well as meaning. Dante picks out with approval items from standard *stilnovo* usage such as *gentile*, *amore*, and *dolcezza* and rejects dialect, conversational idiom, and concrete vocabulary generally. At a very general level all this might account for Dante saying to Virgil, when they first meet at the start of the *Comedy*, that he is the master from whom he learnt 'lo bello stilo che m'ha fatto onore' (*Inf.* 1.87: 'the beautiful style that has brought me honour').

The *De vulgari eloquentia* thus brings home that for Dante inspiration, or following the dictates of love, is at most a starting point for the writing of poetry. There is always the technical issue of suiting style to subject matter and this, Dante insists in the treatise, is hard work: 'hic opus et labor est' ('here is the task and the work'), he says, slightly misquoting Virgil (*Aeneid* 6.129). Poetry requires intellect, technique, and knowledge (2.4.10); in the *Convivio* he says that it involves the skills of the grammarian, the rhetorician, and, because poetry depends on rhythm, the musician (2.10). When he meets Guinizelli in Purgatory he has him acknowledge Arnaut Daniel's technical superiority by terming him 'il miglior fabbro del parlar materno' (*Purg.* 26.117: 'the better smith of the mother tongue'), a phrase which T. S. Eliot takes up in his dedication of the *Waste Land* to Ezra Pound. Even when he is most inspired, Dante is aware of being an artist who thinks hard about his craft and about his own past practice, constantly making his poetry say and do more than it has previously.

The *Comedy*

There are, however, enormous differences between *De vulgari eloquentia* and the poetry it singles out, and Dante's practice and thought in the *Comedy*, for the rules elaborated in the treatise only fit the *Comedy* in a strictly limited way. The hendecasyllable is used throughout, but in the new *terza rima* structure that Dante himself invented. Classical models of construction recommended in the treatise are followed in many ways and much more evidently than before; but the poem's content is quite different from that of classical poetry, and partly as a result its vocabulary vastly exceeds the limited and refined terminology prescribed for the tragic style. In contrast to the strict distinctions of the treatise, and indeed to the standards of classical poetry, the *Comedy* is an extraordinary linguistic hybrid. A conflation of the tragic and comic styles and much more besides, it undermines the theoretical distinction that the treatise makes between them, and, as in the case of allegory, exceeds the conceptual framework that Dante had brought to bear.

We cannot be sure how Dante himself classified the poem, or what title he gave it. The letter to Can Grande calls it a comedy, not on stylistic grounds but on grounds of plot: the progression from Hell to Paradise leads to the happy ending typical of comedies in the traditional sense. Conversely the letter defines tragedy as a form that begins well and ends badly, as traditional tragedies do. In *Inferno* the poem is twice called a comedy (*comedìa*: 16.128 and 21.2), in clear contrast with Virgil's reference, a few lines before the second occasion, to 'l'alta mia tragedìa' (20.113), a reference which must be style- rather than plot-related, since the *Aeneid* does not end badly. Perhaps with the letter in mind, the first commentators refer to the *Comoedia Dantis* or the *Comedia di Dante*, and their title will become the norm, with the adjective *Divina* added from the mid-16th century. Modern critics have tended to stress the stylistic implications, arguing that Dante saw the language of his poem as a sort of expanded version of the middle style, freely and dynamically absorbing into itself the high and low extremes, and thus with a far broader range than the more narrowly elevated vocabulary of the *Aeneid*.

In any case Dante's assessment of the nature and status of his work may well have changed as the poem progressed. It is described as the 'sacrato poema' and the 'poema sacro' at two points well into *Paradiso* (23.62 and 25.1). The word 'poema' indicates a poem of the grandest and most eminent sort, the supreme example of which in Dante's eyes was the *Aeneid*. In effect Dante is now proclaiming that his own work is a poem in the same league, with the added quality of being 'sacro' or 'sacrato' ('sacred' or 'made sacred'), something that the pagan Virgil could never have achieved. As a poet, and in other ways that we shall discuss later, Virgil has been absorbed and superseded, and with him the rest of ancient poetry. In the *Comedy* Virgil serves as a model largely at a general level, as the poet who had described a visit to the underworld in *Aeneid* 6, and who best exemplified the classical high style that Dante modifies and adapts for his own purposes. While he is a major presence as a character, specific echoes of lines and images or techniques are limited in number. The verses that echo Virgil are recastings, images are presented in a new light, and techniques such as the extended simile, which Dante had barely touched before, are deployed with a precision and complexity that Virgil never aspired to.

We used the term realism earlier of the content of the *Comedy*, meaning the concrete, specific, and visual clarity of its representation of the next life. This sort of realism is necessarily an effect of language as well as content, and depends in large part on the enormous range of vocabulary in the poem, particularly its tendency to concreteness and its frequent closeness to everyday life. It is here that the *Comedy* departs most markedly from classical models and from the precepts of the *De vulgari eloquentia*. Large numbers of words appear in the poem that the treatise explicitly excludes from its version of the tragic style, such as *mamma*, used four times, or the kind of dialectal usage that the treatise dismissed as municipal. At times the language of *Inferno* becomes familiar, even earthy, deploying devices and idioms from contemporary *poesia giocosa*. The extreme example comes when Dante and Virgil are escorted for a short while by a bunch of boisterous, loud-mouthed devils, whose leader Malacoda ('Evil tail': all have similarly grotesque names) gives the rest an unusual signal to set off: 'ed elli avea del cul fatto trombetta' (21.139: 'and he had made his arse a trumpet'). The tone teeters here on the edge of comedy in the familiar sense, and the language proved coarse enough to offend the classicizing taste of the Renaissance and after. But it is an exception: there is very little of Shakespeare's bawdy in the *Comedy*. After *Inferno* the low touches there are come at denunciatory moments, such as *bordello* ('brothel') in the address to Italy in Purgatory, and the more latinate *cloaca* ('sewer') in St Peter's diatribe in Paradise against the contemporary Church (*Purg.* 6.18, *Par.* 27.25).

The closeness of at least some of the *Comedy*'s language to everyday usage is one reason why it can seem so modern, especially to anglophone readers. Yet Dante's tone is prevailingly a high and serious one; it is important not to overemphasize its colloquial or demotic aspects, which are only one element in an extraordinary range of vocabulary that also includes the language of the love lyric, a great many terms of a scientific or scholarly, usually Latinate nature, and a considerable number of others that Dante invented himself. *Paradiso* in particular contains a series of conspicuous, mannered, and highly evocative Latinisms appropriate to the sublimity of its subject, though not all Dante's inventions are modelled on Latin. There are also, for example, striking moments in the Heaven of Venus when Italian pronouns are turned into verbs: so 'Già non attendere' io tua dimanda, | s'io m'intuassi come tu m'immii' (9.80–1: approximately 'I would not wait for your request, | if I entered into you in the way you enter into me'); linguistic invention is made the exact correlative of the interpenetration of souls to which Dante aspires here. Italian scholars have used the term *plurilinguismo* to describe the lexically hybrid character of the poem, and the way in which its vast range of vocabulary is merged with other devices and features to create a new kind of high style—a style which, it has been argued, owes as much to the Bible, no stranger to linguistic realism, as it does to Virgil.

6. Roberto Benigni reciting Dante. This performance in Piazza Santa Croce in Florence in 2006 was part of a campaign by the comedian to persuade more people to read Dante. Behind is the statue of Dante erected in 1865 to mark the sixth centenary of his birth.

One of the distinctive features of the *Comedy* is the frequent use of extended similes, some occupying four or more tercets. Dante's narrative is generally rapid and quite concise, compared with that of later verse in the high style, that of Milton for instance. His extended similes, like their classical models, are elements in the narrative that slow it down, thereby contributing to the overall effect of epic dignity. They also tend to have a strongly visual and often realistic character, representing the unfamiliar events and figures of the afterlife in terms familiar to readers, with emotive dimensions as well, which add to the complexity of feeling evoked by a particular episode. When Virgil breaks off a branch from the barren tree in which the soul of the suicide Pier della Vigna is imprisoned, the stump is said to leak blood and words, in the same way as a green twig put on a fire hisses at one end and spurts vapour at the other (*Inf.* 13.40–2). It is a remarkable pictorial image but also one that expresses the horror of the barren vegetable state to which the soul has been reduced or has reduced himself. Images like these are quickly grasped and are particularly frequent in *Inferno*. In later parts of the poem pictorial images can be much more complex and quite often demand considerable effort and knowledge on the part of the reader. Even *Inferno* can deploy names or episodes from the Bible or ancient poetry and history in its similes, usually in a periphrastic and allusive way. When Dante and Virgil look down to see Ulysses and other false counsellors enveloped in tongues of flame below them, Dante draws an evocative and slightly mysterious comparison with fireflies watched by a peasant from a hillside at harvest time. The flames are then immediately compared in a second simile to the flame that 'he who avenged himself with the bears' saw in the sky when the chariot carried Elijah up into Heaven (*Inf.* 26.34–9). We have to know our biblical prophets well enough here to identify the first figure as Elisha, and even then we may wonder about the exact significance of the image, beyond increasing the suspense, giving a certain grandeur to the writing, and possibly suggesting the parallel with Dante's own ascent to Paradise. *Paradiso* has even more elaborate similes, which we will discuss in our final chapter.

Periphrasis, personification, repetition, apostrophes, and
rhetorical questions are among the many poetic figures that Dante
derived from ancient literature and to some extent from the
medieval Latin tradition, and used systematically to raise his
language to a level comparable in its own way to that of the
classical high style. None of these had been used except cursorily
and occasionally by previous authors writing in Italian, or for that
matter in French or Provençal. The device most extensively used
by Dante, and the most flexible and distinctive, is metaphor. The
Comedy's metaphors tend to be concrete and brief, typically
consisting in one word only: unlike the extended similes, ornate
extended metaphors are fairly rare. Many take the form of verbs,
and have a characteristic tendency to express abstract, causal, or
circumstantial connections in terms of direct physical action: for
instance 'lamenti saettaron me diversi' (*Inf.* 29.43: 'different
laments arrowed [through] me'); and famously when Francesca
says 'Per più fiate gli occhi ci sospinse | quella lettura, e scolorocci
il viso' (*Inf.* 5.130–1: literally 'Several times that reading pushed
our eyes together | and paled our faces'). Metaphors can be given a
striking prominence by their position at the end of the line in
rhyme, with effects which it is usually impossible to reproduce in
translation. The following is a particularly strong example; it
describes the purification in Purgatory of the slothful, who make
up for their former lives by chasing at top speed around the
mountain:

> cotal per quel giron suo passo *falca*
> per quel ch'io vidi di color, venendo,
> cui buon volere e giusto amor *cavalca*.
> [such [a throng] *scythed* its way around that circle,
> as I could see when it came,
> of those whom right will and just love *ride*.]

(Purg. 18.94–6)

'Scythed' and 'ride' give characteristically vigorous and physical
expression to the passionate desire that drives the souls on. In
such metaphors there is a disproportion, by the standards of

normal parlance, between the metaphorical vehicle and its tenor or meaning. The effect is to heighten as well as elevate Dante's realism, emphasizing not just the visual aspect of things, but giving force and obtrusive immediacy to both inner and outer experience.

While verse structure and metre receive great attention in the *De vulgari eloquentia*, neither there nor anywhere else does Dante say anything about *terza rima*, the units of three lines, sometimes called *terzine* or tercets, into which the 100 canti of the *Comedy* are divided. Though the individual line continues to be the hendecasyllable (see Box 2), the way Dante binds the lines together has no real precedent, though scholars have pointed to some Provençal forms or even to the rhyme patterns in the second part of a sonnet. The first rhyme in the canto appears only twice, while subsequent rhymes are used three times in an alternating pattern (ABA BCB CDC...). A new rhyme is introduced in the middle line of each tercet, until the canto is rounded off (generally around 140 lines later) by a final line rhyming with the middle rhyme of the tercet before (...WXW XYX YZY Z). *Terza rima* thus imparts a strong forward movement to the canto, by ensuring that each tercet is linked by rhyme both to the group before and to the group after. Some see in the pattern a reflection of the Holy Trinity; whether or not that is so, *terza rima* makes the poem easier to memorize, and binds its texture together. It is also one reason why the text of the *Comedy* proved from the beginning remarkably stable in comparison with many others from the Middle Ages, even though we have no manuscript in Dante's own hand. Given the rhyme-scheme, it is almost impossible to take out lines or to insert them at all convincingly. It is also a scheme which is very much Dante's, at least for serious poetry. It will continue to be used throughout the Renaissance but almost always for conversational or satirical verse.

The *terzina* shapes the poem's syntax, and is in turn supported by it. Again Dante owes a great deal to classical example. Taking up the elaborate mode of sentence construction used in Latin prose as well as poetry, Dante's sentences are complex structures with a proliferation of subordinate clauses, and a strong emphasis on connections between sentences as well as within them. Within the *terzina* the vast majority of lines are end-stopped: the line-end coincides with the end of a clause or at least the end of a phrase, and *enjambement*, in which the end of the line occurs in the middle of a phrase, is comparatively rare. Conversely only a minute number of sentence-breaks or other major syntactic divisions occur in the middle of a line. More distinctively, the major syntactic divisions regularly fall at the end of the three-line unit, with very few sentence endings in the first or second lines of the *terzina*: sentences consist as a rule of three lines of verse or of multiples of three. Syntactical complexity thus combines with rhythmical balance, contributing significantly to the overall effect of epic dignity. That effect is particularly marked in the sentences that span two or more *terzine*, of which there are about ten per canto on average. These increase in number as the poem progresses, raising the level of the style and slowing the rhythm.

Rhyming can be relatively easy in Italian because of the large number of recurrent suffixes in the language, such as the infinitive -*are*, or the past participle -*ato*. Popular verse commonly uses rhymes of this sort, but in Dante they are relatively rare, especially in the *Comedy*. Dante is extraordinarily inventive in the number of different combinations of sounds that he deploys in rhyme, far more so than later Italian writers of long narrative poems, with the possible exception of Torquato Tasso in the 16th century. About a third of the rhymes are used only once, and significant numbers of new ones are introduced from one *cantica* to the next. Range and difficulty are accompanied by freedom and inventiveness. A large proportion of the word-forms in rhyme position do not appear at all in other positions in the line, many more than in later poets or in Dante's own lyric poetry. Given the absence of a standard language, he was free to take much greater linguistic liberties than his successors. But rhyme was not just a technical challenge; it was also the means for creating effects of emphasis and surprise: the bold and expressive metaphors looked at above are made all the more forceful by the rare *-alca* rhyme.

Such effects disrupt the regularity of the poem's syntax and metre in a way that seems to reflect the challenges and uncertainties of its meanings. On the one hand, regularity in the language reflects the symmetrical architecture of the content: the division of the souls into categories in each *cantica*, for instance; the distribution of guardians in the circles of Hell; the examples of virtue and vice, beatitudes and dreams in Purgatory; the choreographed movements of the blessed in Paradise. In fact the whole poem becomes, as we shall see in the following chapters, a celebration of the underlying order of the universe and its source in the mind of God. On the other hand repetition always includes variation and order is constantly challenged, in the detailed fabric of the poem as well as through the major questions of interpretation it raises.

For its translators the *Comedy*'s formal features are a major problem. *Terza rima* is hard in English, and the ways Dante exploits it are generally impossible to render. Dorothy Sayers and Barbara Reynolds managed to keep the triple rhymes in their mid-20th century Penguin versions, but at the cost of considerable contortion. Most of their successors have opted ruefully for the unrhymed route, though Clive James made an idiosyncratic return to rhyming (not in formal *terza rima*) in his 2013 version. The distinctive features of the *Comedy*'s language are just as problematic in translations. Recently (most strikingly in Steve Ellis's version) there has been a tendency to opt for a popular idiom, which may be a healthy corrective to the Miltonic sonorities of Henry Cary and Henry Wadsworth Longfellow, the most widely read 19th century translators of Dante into English, but leaves a great deal out of account. Ideally a translator will balance the realistic and the everyday with the general tendency to elevation of tone and register that runs through the whole poem, and becomes increasingly the norm in *Purgatorio* and *Paradiso*.

Most translators would acknowledge that this is likely to remain a
pipe-dream. The result, though, seems to be not so much one of
despair as an ever renewed sense of urgency. There have been
more than fifty English versions of the whole *Comedy* since a first
complete translation of *Inferno* was published in 1782, and they
keep on coming.

Chapter 5
Humanity

> Quanto ragion qui vede,
> dir ti poss'io; da indi in là t' aspetta
> pur a Beatrice, ch'è opra di fede
> [All that reason sees here
> I can tell you; beyond wait
> until Beatrice, for it is the task of faith]
>
> (*Purg.* 18.46–8)

Reason and faith

What it means to be human, and what the purpose is of human existence, are questions Dante comes back to again and again. They are first articulated in the *Convivio*; a good deal of what he says there will resurface in the *Comedy* and in the *Monarchia*, but it is in the *Convivio* that the celebration of human qualities is most vigorous and forthright. Aristotle is the authority he appeals to and whose texts he most cites: the ancient Greek philosopher is the 'master and leader of human reason' (4.6.8) who in the *Comedy* becomes the 'maestro di color che sanno' (*Inf.* 4.131: 'the master of those that know'). Like virtually all his contemporaries, Dante could only read Aristotle in medieval Latin translations, often based on Arabic versions. These had been taken up by the most advanced Christian thinkers of the 13th century, in particular Thomas Aquinas, who had died in 1274, nine years after

Dante's birth, and some of whose work he certainly knew. How much of Aristotle Dante actually read, and whether he read in full the works he cites, is hard to tell. What we can be sure of is that Aristotle is fundamental to his culture. The *Convivio* opens by citing the first sentence of the *Metaphysics* ('All men desire to know'), though it is the *Ethics* that he will draw on most.

The *Convivio* takes from the *Ethics* the definition of reason as the essential property of humanity, and the related argument that the end of life, and the source of true happiness for human beings, is to fulfil their rational capacity through the pursuit of knowledge and virtue. This in turn assumes that morality consists in the control of action through reason, which in Aristotle's view means choosing the middle way between a series of opposite extremes, an ethics of moderation in which not only lustfulness, greed, and wrath are vices, for example, but also New Testament virtues such as abstinence and humility. Aristotle's ethics were secular in this way and also social: human beings live, and find their fulfilment, with their fellows in civil society. The *Convivio* is addressed to men playing an active role in the world; in the fourth book Dante argues that nobility is a matter of virtue, not inherited social position and wealth, and draws up a list of specific virtues that is substantially Aristotelian. These fall into two types, the intellectual virtues involved in the pursuit of knowledge, and the moral virtues that govern the life of action in the world. Either can lead to happiness. The happiness that the former lead to is superior, since knowledge is superior to action, as Aristotle also believed; but knowledge is necessarily imperfect while in the body, and will only be complete in Heaven. Dante insists that moral perfection, on the other hand, is fully achievable in our life here below, since human reason is the only necessary foundation for leading a good life. Significantly, religious observation is only included in the *Convivio*'s list of virtues as a requisite for old age, in preparation for death.

This very secular ethics was unusual though not unprecedented for Dante's time. Similar ideas seem to have been in the air in contemporary Florence, and were put forward in the previous century in Paris. But the more orthodox position was that of Thomas Aquinas, that while the rational ethics of Aristotle were good, the spiritual ethics of the New Testament were better. Dante's more radical solution makes the two spheres of reason and religion separate and independent: happiness in this life is one thing, and is pursued through the exercise of reason; happiness in the next life is another, and is pursued under the aegis of religion. This dualism, appearing first in the *Convivio*, is the basis of Dante's distinction between the roles of Emperor and Pope that we referred to in Chapter 3, and will return to again in Chapter 5: mankind is led to earthly happiness by the Emperor under the guidance of reason, and to heavenly happiness by the Pope under the guidance of scripture. Yet Dante's theorizing in this regard is conducted at a very high level of abstraction, and leaves some significant gaps. How human beings should actually live their lives from one day to the next is left unclear: the implication that they should pursue heavenly and earthly happiness simultaneously ignores potential conflicts between the two concepts. For instance, the theory seems to leave out of account the question of monastic life. Much of *Paradiso* 10–13 focuses on Saints Francis and Dominic and the decadence of the orders they founded. Monks have to follow the spiritual ethics of the New Testament, not the worldly ethics of Aristotle. To judge from the *Comedy*, where the idea of the two goals of life is still vigorously maintained, Dante must have found some way of reconciling his Aristotelian idea of earthly happiness with monastic renunciation, but we do not know what it was.

In fact there is a religious foundation, and often a religious colouring, even to the boldest secular moments of the *Convivio* and the *Monarchia*. Dante is not an Enlightenment thinker who bets all on analytic or scientific thinking of a modern kind. Reason is an image of the divine mind implanted in us directly by God when the soul is created. If rightly used, it can tell us truths that conform with or anticipate the truths of Christianity, beginning with the existence of the Divinity in some form or other and the immortality of the human soul. It also tells us about realities of the phenomenal world, including nature and the cosmos, though its primary province is moral philosophy; Dante is polemically opposed to abstruse metaphysical speculation of the kind practised in the universities, particularly Paris. Reason has strict limits. As the *Convivio* argues, truths that are the specific province of Christianity can only be known through faith (3.15.6); the mystery of the Trinity would be the foremost example. The principle is strongly underlined in the *Comedy* and, as we have seen, is implicit in Dante's choice of guides. The point is made explicitly in the lines at the head of this chapter: whatever is available to man's natural reason belongs to Virgil, the knowledge that only Christian faith can bring belongs to Beatrice. Since Virgil is guiding Dante to Beatrice, the implication is that in Dante's thinking reason and rational knowledge, broadly speaking philosophy, prepare the ground for the coming of faith and the knowledge associated with it, broadly speaking theology. Reason and faith are complementary, not opposed or divergent, as they were often thought to be in the Middle Ages, and as they usually are thought to be now. As Virgil explains in Purgatory, the error of classical thinkers, including Aristotle, was to think they could understand the matters that properly belong to faith (*Purg.* 3.34–45). There is an obvious connection here with the journey of Ulysses, a graphic example of the ancients' refusal to recognize the divinely imposed limits on human knowledge.

The moral system of *Inferno*

Dante's guide through a Christian Hell is a pagan poet. The choice of Virgil rather than of Aristotle or any other philosopher stems from the esteem and love Dante has for the Roman poet and his work, as is immediately made plain in *Inferno* 1. Narratively it is justified by the knowledge of the afterlife shown in Virgil's account of Aeneas' visit to the underworld in *Aeneid* 6, supplemented by a story (*Inf.* 9.22–30), which Dante may have invented, of the witch

Erichtho transporting Virgil's soul down to the depths of Hell in order to extract an unnamed soul. But in choosing Virgil to guide him, Dante echoes and extends his view that the most exalted sides of ancient culture accord with and anticipate Christian belief. While the gods and goddesses were false and the stories in which they figure untrue, the greatest ancient poetry, like Aristotelian philosophy and science, contains important moral messages and truths about the world generally. Virgil in the *Comedy* is a good and knowledgeable guide, though at various moments he needs divine help or has to appeal to divine authority for the journey he and Dante are making. It may still be surprising to find him as a pagan explaining to Dante the principles on which Hell is organized. He does this in *Inferno* 11, when he and Dante have paused on the far edge of the sixth circle in order for Dante to get used to the stench that comes up from the lower reaches (see Box 3).

Virgil begins with the three circles they have still to visit. These are all circles of malice, willing the harm of others, which, appealing to a distinction in Cicero, Virgil divides between violence and fraud: violence is less serious because it only abuses powers which we share with the beasts, whereas fraud is an abuse of our specifically human faculty, reason. Violence is punished in Circle 7, fraud in Circles 8 and 9, the latter being then divided between fraud against other people in general, and fraud that breaks a special bond, in other words treachery. All three circles are further subdivided. Circle 7 has three *gironi*, each of which in turn contains two complementary categories of sin: first, violence to others and their property, second violence to oneself and one's own property, and third violence against God and his property, nature. Circle 8, later to be called Malebolge from the *bolge* (*bolgia* means 'sack' or 'pocket') into which it is divided, includes ten sub-categories that Virgil lists here; Circle 9 has four. To explain how the upper circles (2–5) fit into this scheme, Virgil switches to the distinction in Aristotle's *Ethics* between incontinence, fraud, and 'bestiality', and, without explaining what 'bestiality' means, assigns lust, gluttony, avarice and

Box 3 The moral system and structure of Hell

Circle	Sins	Figures
Vestibule	Pusillanimous	
1 Limbo	Virtuous pagans, unbaptized children	Aristotle, Homer, Ovid, Lucan, Saladin, Averroes, Avicenna
Sins of incontinence (2-5)		Charon, Minos
2	Lustful	Paolo and Francesca
3	Gluttons	Ciacco
4	Avaricious and prodigals	Plutus
5	Wrathful	Filippo Argenti
City of Dis (6-9)		
6	Heretics	Farinata, Frederick II
7 Sins of violence		
Girone 1	Murderers and robbers	
Girone 2	Suicides and squanderers	Pier della Vigna
Girone 3	Violent against God	Capaneus
	Sodomites and usurers	Brunetto Latini
8 Sins of fraud against others in general (Malebolge)		Gerione
Bolgia 1	Panders and seducers	
Bolgia 2	Flatterers	
Bolgia 3	Simoniacs (corrupt clergy)	Nicholas III
Bolgia 4	Sorcerers and astrologers	
Bolgia 5	Barrators (corrupt politicians)	Devils
Bolgia 6	Hypocrites	Frati godenti, Caiaphas
Bolgia 7	Thieves	Vanni Fucci
Bolgia 8	False counsellors	Ulysses, Guido da Montefeltro
Bolgia 9	Sowers of discord	Muhammad, Alì, Bertran de Born, Mosca dei Lamberti
Bolgia 10	Counterfeiters	
9 Sins of fraud through treachery		Giants
Caina	Traitors to family	
Antenora	Political traitors	Ugolino, Archbishop Ruggieri
Tolomea	Traitors to guests	
Giudecca	Traitors to their lords	Satan, Judas, Brutus, Cassius

prodigality, and wrath to incontinence. This means allowing reason to be overcome by desire, and is less serious, and therefore punished less severely, than willing the harm of others. We thus arrive at a scheme that provides a rationale for most of Hell and that centres on insufficient use or deliberate misuse of our human powers.

We may still be scratching our heads over some issues. The Aristotelian and Ciceronian parts are hard to reconcile with each other, the order of exposition is back to front, and there are important gaps. The one and only clear example in Hell of the Aristotelian view of virtue as the middle path between two extremes is the avaricious and the prodigal, put together in Circle 4. Malebolge, dealt with very rapidly by Virgil, actually takes up nearly a third of the whole *Inferno*, and its ten subdivisions seem to have no particular order. We can guess why the heretics, the term used to mean those who do not believe in the immortality of the soul, are where they are in Circle 6, since they abused their reason, but are not so bad as the violent or the fraudulent in the circles below. Yet the somewhat rickety pagan scheme Virgil is proposing has nothing to say about this category, nor can it ever. For Dante's Hell remains fundamentally Christian: it is the state of being without God, and the form it takes is a parody of the heavenly city, a complicated, divided, and deeply flawed place, made all the more dysfunctional by the earthquake which occurred at the moment of Christ's death on the cross and wrecked some of its internal walls. Ultimately, therefore, Hell is also irrational, because it is beyond the full comprehension of our divinely implanted reason, while at the same time being part of divine creation. The paradox is traditional and difficult. When Dante looks up at the gate of Hell and sees the inscription telling those who enter to abandon all hope, he reads that hell was made by 'the divine power, the highest wisdom and the primal love' (*Inf.* 3.5–6), and immediately says to Virgil that the sense of the words is hard. The rest of the poem will do little to clarify how these obviously positive virtues of an omnipotent God were responsible for Hell, even if that must be the case.

A still clearer challenge to Dante's, and the reader's, understanding is presented by the topmost circle of Hell, also left out of Virgil's categories, and the one in which he himself resides: Limbo is where the souls of the virtuous pagans and the unbaptized children are located. As Virgil says to Dante (*Inf.* 4.34), none of them sinned; they are there only because they lacked Christian faith, and their only suffering is a hopeless desire for the God that they did not know on earth. Within Limbo special treatment is reserved for the great figures of antiquity: Aristotle, Virgil, and other ancient philosophers, poets, and heroes reside in a 'noble castle' enclosing a luminous green field, which contrasts sharply with the horrific landscape to come. Their eternal exclusion from salvation is tragic, but Dante's respect and admiration for their human qualities and virtues is evident, for his conception of Limbo rests on the firm principle that it is possible to be wholly good outside the Christian religion through the proper exercise of reason alone. Like many other Christian rationalists, therefore, Dante cannot help trying to understand the apparent injustices of divine providence. How can virtuous human beings be damned solely because they lived, like Virgil, 'at the time of the false lying gods' (*Inf.* 1.72)? We shall see later how the problem refuses to go away even in *Paradiso*.

Since it is possible to be wholly good morally without being a Christian, it is not surprising (though it may have been so for his contemporaries) to find Dante including among residents of Limbo the Arab philosophers Averroes and Avicenna and the 11th century Sultan Saladin, mythicized as a noble and courtly ruler throughout Western Europe (*Inf.* 4.129 and 143–4). That does not mean Dante is tolerant of other religions: he has no doubts about the rightness of the Crusades and the duty of Christian rulers to fight unbelievers rather than each other. Muhammad and his nephew Alì are treated as Christian heretics and put amongst the sowers of discord in Malebolge, while the Hebrew priest Caiaphas and the others who pressed for Christ's execution are damned as hypocrites in *Inferno* 23. Like his early commentators, Dante probably knew nothing of Islam, and his main concern regarding Judaism is understanding the providential punishment of the Jews for the crucifixion of Christ, which is discussed at length in *Paradiso*. In these respects he stays very much within the limits of medieval Christianity.

Humanity in *Inferno*

If sin in *Inferno* is a failure or misuse of reason, then, according to Dante's thinking, it necessarily entails a loss of humanity. This is graphically represented in the manifold ways in which sins are punished. Although pain is never forgotten, and Virgil implies (*Inf.* 11.27) that the punishments are more severe the further down a sinner is in Hell, the stress is more on the correspondence between the punishment and the sin. Dante himself gives us a term for this when, among the sowers of discord, he meets the Provençal troubadour Bertran de Born, punished for fomenting the feud between the English King Henry II and his son. Holding up his head like a lantern, Bertran declares that he demonstrates the principle of *contrapasso* (*Inf.* 28. 142), literally 'retaliation'; just as he separated the king and his son, so his own head is separated from his body. This sort of analogical or metaphorical relationship between punishment and sin seems to obtain in all the circles of Hell, though sometimes the connections are specific, sometimes more general, indirect, or open-ended. The lustful are blown around by a tempest, as they were by their passion, the suicides are deprived of their bodies, as they deprived themselves of life. The thieves are metamorphosed into reptiles and back into human beings, a metaphor for the generally bestial nature of sin which may also point to their refusal to adhere to fundamental distinctions of ownership, and indirectly to the primal theft of the apple instigated by the serpent Satan. Overall the punishments in Malebolge, the first circle of fraud, are much more physically repellent and involve much greater violence to the human form than those in the circles above, whilst at the very bottom of Hell, where the traitors are punished, the sinners are deprived of most aspects of life by being buried motionless in ice, unable even to weep. Their humanity has literally been frozen out of them.

Satan himself, 'lo 'mperador del doloroso regno' (*Inf.* 34.28: 'the Emperor of the suffering realm'), only has the power to send out the wind that freezes the souls with his enormous bat-like wings, and to chew with his three mouths on the three signal traitors to Christ and the Roman Empire, Judas, Brutus, and Cassius. The extreme form of evil to which all other forms of evil tend, and which does in a sense determine them, is for Dante ugly, deformed, immense, mechanical, and without language. It is as close to mere matter as an immortal being can become. Earlier on inhumanity had also been graphically represented in the various guardians who administer Hell, all in varying ways prefigurations of Lucifer and mostly of classical derivation, now made monstrous and grotesque. Virgil's Minos, for instance, dispenses justice as the Cretan king he was in life; in Dante he is a snarling bestial figure who indicates to the souls which circle they are condemned to by the number of times he winds his tail around himself (*Inf.* 5.1–15). He at least can speak intelligibly. Plutus, the classical god of riches, becomes a wolf-like beast shouting Satan's name in a non-language (*Inf.* 7.1), and other similar guardians will tend to have no language at all. The giants that guard the cliff between Malebolge and the circle of treachery are massive, horrible, speechless shapes. The devils in the *bolgia* of the barrators still have language, but their grotesque lack of humanity is signalled by their leader making 'his arse a trumpet' (*Inf.* 21.139) as they set off on their escort mission.

The sinners suffer because the choices they made in life have determined what they are, irredeemably since they have not repented. Their understanding of other possible ways of living, even of having abused the divine power of reason granted to them, is either non-existent or limited to a sense of having lost something they can apprehend only very imperfectly. Instead they embrace their condition, whatever the pain involved, hurrying to enter Charon's boat to be transported to their particular place of torment, and once there finding a strange kind of fulfilment in being for ever what they were in life, like the existentialist heroes of Sartre. The torments thus become representations not merely of the sin, but of what they are. The defiant claim of the blasphemer Capaneus, punished for having defied Jupiter at the gates of Thebes, speaks for all his fellow sinners: 'Qual io fui vivo, tal son morto' (*Inf.* 14.51: 'As I was in life, so I am in death'). Paradoxically, the real losers and self-destroyers are the endless streams of souls just inside the gates of Hell: the pusillanimous, mentioned only to be left outside the poem and its whole system, 'a Dio spiacenti e a' nemici sui' (*Inf.* 3.63: 'displeasing to God and to his enemies'), because they refused to make the choices that human beings cannot avoid if they are to be human.

Many sinners are openly condemned or openly invite condemnation from the reader. When Dante reacts with personal loathing to the Florentine sinner Filippo Argenti, Virgil embraces him warmly (*Inf.* 8.44–5): his spontaneous reaction and God's judgement happily coincide. There will be other similar instances later, but again and again his reactions are more complicated and at times plainly discrepant with divine justice. Virgil upbraids him fiercely for showing a criminal compassion, when he finds himself weeping over the paralytic distortion of the human form imposed on sorcerers and the like (*Inf.* 20.28–30); nevertheless the offence to his sense of the human is plain. In the most striking and moving encounters the humanity still present in the sinners themselves is highlighted in complex and often positive ways, though with at least a measure of ambiguity that readers have to resolve for themselves. We have already discussed Ulysses, Brunetto, and Francesca, none of whom can be straightforwardly condemned. In each case the main focus of the episode in which they appear seems to shift away from the sin towards human values which Dante admires or sympathizes with, so that we have to decide for ourselves how there might nevertheless be parallels between the encounter and the punishment. Similar complexities arise with the suicide Pier della Vigna (*Inf.* 13) and the false counsellor Guido da Montefeltro (*Inf.* 27). Perhaps the most striking example is the heretic Farinata degli Uberti, who pushes himself up above the edge of the sarcophagus-like tomb in which he lies, 'com' avesse l'inferno a gran dispitto' (*Inf.* 10.36: 'as if he held Hell in great scorn'). Ulysses seems one sort of solitary hero, and Farinata another; we shall return to his virtues and his limits in the next chapter.

The last of the great human episodes of *Inferno* is one which English readers have been particularly drawn to since Chaucer first adapted it in his 'Monk's Tale', and which Seamus Heaney translated with the internecine violence of 1970s Northern Ireland in mind. At the end of canto 32, at the very bottom of Hell, where the traitors are buried in ice, Dante is struck by the revolting sight of a sinner gnawing the brain of another. At the start of the next canto the sinner raises his head, wiping his mouth on the other's hair to tell his story: he is Ugolino della Gherardesca, a Pisan aristocrat who, as a result of factional struggles, was imprisoned in a tower with his sons and starved to death by his enemy and now victim, the Archbishop Ruggieri degli Ubaldini. The pathos is extreme: Ugolino narrates how his sons begged him for help and even offered themselves to be eaten, then how they died one by one, and he was left blinded by hunger, groping to find their bodies until he himself finally succumbed (feeding himself, some have argued, on his children). Even more than in the Brunetto episode, there is a remarkable contrast here between the human pathos of Ugolino's narrative, and the inhuman, in this case quite bestial, context, emphasized again at the end of his story, when he once more clenches his teeth into the skull of Ruggieri, like a dog seizing on a bone (see Figure 7).

Dante did not know Aristotle's *Poetics*, but horror and pity, which Aristotle declares fundamental to tragedy, are here in abundance. What Dante does not allow for is any kind of catharsis. The narrative is followed by a denunciation of Pisa for its brutal involvement of innocent children in the punishment inflicted on Ugolino. Then Dante moves on, as he had moved on from all the

7. Alberto Martini, Ugolino and the Archbishop Ruggieri (*Inferno* 33), from the set of illustrations to the *Divine Comedy* created by Martini between 1901 and 1944.

other episodes. At least for him, if not for all his readers, it is by going further and coming to see things in different ways that solutions can be envisaged to the dilemmas and problems which Hell has posed—though as we shall see the solutions are by no means complete.

Humanity in *Purgatorio*

The torments in Purgatory work quite differently from those in Hell and have a much clearer rationale. The souls have all repented before death of their sinful actions, and are now purging themselves of wrongful desires, or rather, since they can no longer sin, of the traces which wrongful desires and actions have left in them. Purgatory thus gradually frees the saved souls from the negative aspects of their earthly humanity, whereas Hell perpetuates the earthly humanity of the souls who have not repented. The sufferings may be almost as terrible as those of the damned, but the penitents eagerly submit to them, not because they define them, as was the case in Hell, but because they are the means to achieving heavenly bliss. The process of purgation may take hundreds of years and may include periods on various terraces of the mountain (see Box 4); once it is complete, the mountain shakes and the purified soul is free to ascend to Heaven. Virgil and Dante witness this happening in the case of the poet Statius, who explains the process to them (*Purg.* 21.40–72).

Repentance is the one and only reason why the sinners in Purgatory are not in Hell. This is made clear from the beginning, in Ante-Purgatory, the area near the foot of the mountain where the souls wait who repented of their sins late, or died outside the Church. Along with negligent rulers, they are obliged to delay their entry into Purgatory proper for varying amounts of time to compensate for their failures. Manfred, the illegitimate son of the Holy Roman Emperor Frederick II, was excommunicated by the Pope and died in battle; his sins, were horrible, as he says to Dante (*Purg.* 3.121), but his repentance at the point of death was sufficient to save him, even though he was excluded from the sacraments of the Church. Similarly the Ghibelline leader Bonconte da Montefeltro recounts his salvation at the point of death in the Battle of Campaldino simply on account of 'una lagrimetta' (5.107:

Box 4 The moral system and structure of Purgatory

Places	Categories and events	Figures
Shoreline	New arrivals	Casella
Antepurgatory		
	Excommunicates	Manfred
	Indolent	Belacqua
	Late repentant	Bonconte da Montefeltro
	Neglectful rulers	Sordello, Currado Malaspina, Nino Visconti, Rudolph
Terraces of Purgatory		
Cornice 1	Pride	
Cornice 2	Envy	
Cornice 3	Anger	Marco Lombardo
Cornice 4	Sloth	
Cornice 5	Avarice	Statius
Cornice 6	Gluttony	Forese Donati, Bonagiunta da Lucca
Cornice 7	Lust	Guinizelli, Arnaut Daniel
Earthly Paradise	Procession and pageant	Matelda, Beatrice

Humanity

'one little tear') of repentance; conversely his father Guido, the adviser of Boniface VIII, had told Dante in *Inferno* 27 that he was condemned to Hell despite the Pope's absolution of his sins, because the absolution was not accompanied by true repentance. Repentance and hence salvation depend only on the individual's act of will and God's grace; the role of the Church's sacraments is not ultimately decisive one way or the other.

In Purgatory, as we said in Chapter 3, understanding comes to the fore to an extent that it does not in Hell. In keeping with Virgil's statement in the lines at the head of this chapter, the wisdom and knowledge deployed are human and rational; Virgil is still Dante's guide and the pagan poet he was in life. As such he has no direct knowledge of Purgatory and is regularly unsure about the way to take. Yet now, in a way that was barely evident in Hell, he repeatedly shows himself to be the 'famoso saggio' ('famous sage') Dante had called him at their meeting (*Inf.* 1.89). Two of his major speeches (*Purg.* 17 and 18) are on love, viewed now not as erotic desire but as the motive for any human action, good or bad. Love is the desire for the good, and the greatest good is God, but human love can easily be misdirected by 'false images of the good', as Beatrice terms them later (*Purg.* 30.131), when love fails to be controlled by reason. It is on this basis that Purgatory has its order. Wrong love can be directed to the harm of others (purged on the terraces of pride, envy, and wrath), it can be too weakly directed to the good (hence acedia or sloth), or it can become the excessive love of inferior or secondary goods (avarice and prodigality, greed, and lust). We are thus given a clear, orderly, rational presentation of the moral system of Purgatory, set in the context of a larger view of human motivation. It is also a view notable for its consequence, that sin or vice is the result of poor judgement: a remarkably optimistic view of human motivation, and a key element in Dante's conviction of the moral perfectibility of humanity in this life.

Yet Purgatory is a Christian place, staffed by angels and with eminently Christian functions, and the borderlines between Christian and non-Christian are sometimes blurred. Divine support is far more evident than in Hell. Progress up the mountain has a rhythm to it and the various terraces follow repeated patterns. On first entering Purgatory proper Dante's forehead is marked by the Angelic gatekeeper with seven Ps standing for the seven sins (*peccata*) purged on the mountain. As he leaves each terrace, an Angel voices an appropriate Beatitude from Christ's sermon on the Mount, at which one of the Ps is removed, and progress upwards becomes easier. The terraces have near their entrances examples of the virtue opposed to the sin that is purged, and near their exits examples of that sin being punished. The modes of representation vary, and include reliefs, visions, shouted statements; but in each set of examples classical figures and events are mixed with biblical ones, as if the two are complementary. Time also moves forward in an ordered and significant way. Dante and Virgil arrive at dawn on Easter morning and take three days to reach the mountain's summit and the Earthly Paradise. They climb during the day: at night they must rest and further progress is forbidden. Obviously allegory is now much more to the fore, as we discussed in Chapter 3. The sun which shines during the day is an image of the divine light, and night an image of its apparent withdrawal.

Human freedom is the goal to which Dante's and the penitents' ascents are directed. This is not freedom in the sense of a release from social rules or constraints; it is the recovery of lost innocence that vice or the world have undermined or buried, a return to the state of Adam and Eve before the Fall. At the top of the mountain of Purgatory Dante arrives in the biblical Garden of Eden, purified of the wrong love that is the source of every sin. As Virgil says in his last speech, he is no longer needed as a guide: Dante's *arbitrio*, his judgement and will, is now 'free, right and sound' (27.140: 'libero, dritto e sano è tuo arbitrio'), and he should do as it bids him. No longer tainted by erroneous loves, he is free to direct his will towards the greatest good of all, God, and thus to rise effortlessly to Heaven, as he is ready to do at the end of the *cantica*. If we look back, we can see that he has now reached the summit of 'il dilettoso monte | ch'è principio e cagion di tutta gioia' (*Inf.* 1.77–8: 'the delightful mountain | that is the beginning and cause of all joy'), which he was struggling to climb after emerging from the dark wood at the very start of the poem. That wood has been transformed into an idyllic forest where Dante is free to wander, accompanied by a lovely young woman, Matelda, who briefly takes over the role of guide, and seems to be an embodiment of earthly moral perfection. By now the desire for Heaven and the spiritual ethics of the New Testament seem to have the dominant part, not the rational morality of Aristotle.

If Hell is an image of earthly life lived without God, with the strong implication that such is the current state of the world, Purgatory seems to be an image of what the Christian life could or should be. This means that there are almost no equivalents of the dramatic figures who seize our attention in *Inferno*. Isolation, fundamental egocentricity, lack of a moral centre give way to communal feelings rather than personal ones. Souls work and suffer together, hesitating to push themselves forward and assert their individuality. The emphasis is all on shared values, which allow for much less drama than was the case in Hell: friendship for each other and frequently for Dante, concern for those left behind, regret for the current state of the world. This strongly Christian character should not surprise us, since Purgatory is in the next life, not this one. Yet we have to wonder how this narrative of a journey to prelapsarian purity really fits with the idea of reason, or Virgil, guiding Dante to Beatrice, or with the concept of happiness in this life grounded in a worldly and social ethics quite different from that of the Beatitudes. Is the Purgatorial journey an image of a much more Christian journey that all men should go through in their life on earth, or is it something that will only happen in the next life and that, quite exceptionally, has been granted to Dante while he is still among the living? Dante leaves these questions open; the full meaning of the journey through Purgatory, like much else in the *Comedy*, is for the reader to decide.

Nor should we overstate *Purgatorio*'s Christian character: even taken literally, it certainly does not centre exclusively on purgation. It is the *cantica* in which Dante's concern for the state of humanity on earth is most fully developed and articulated, as we shall see in the next chapter. If human means humane and personal, moreover, this is the most human of the three *cantiche*. It contains some of the most evocative nature poetry in the entire *Comedy*. The light and freshness at the foot of the mountain mark a complete change of tone from the darkness of Hell, and will be followed by a series of affecting descriptions of sunset and dawn, in which moods of romantic melancholy and not quite confident anticipation strike touching lyrical chords, all culminating in the idyllic beauty of the 'dense, living divine forest' of the Earthly Paradise (28.2: 'la divina foresta spessa e viva'). Personal friends come to the fore, such as the ironic, half-humorous Belacqua in canto 4, who seems the same lazy individual he was in life, but is now waiting patiently to begin his penance; and Forese Donati in canti 23–4, the companion of Dante's misspent youth, who now berates the rampant immorality of contemporary Florence. Meetings with political leaders and earlier vernacular poets are all rich in human warmth. Above all Dante's relationship with Virgil takes on deeper nuances. We have noted how Dante weeps when Virgil departs, at the start of the most personal episode in the whole *Comedy*, his reunion with Beatrice and the re-evocation of his love for her. The earlier encounter with the 1st century Latin poet Statius highlights both the stature and significance of Virgil's poetry, and the tragedy of his exclusion from Heaven. Statius, whom Dante makes a Christian, compares Virgil to a man carrying a lantern behind his back, lighting the way for those that follow him but not for himself (*Purg.* 22.67–9): Virgil's poetry not only inspired him as a writer but also, through the supposed prophecy of the coming of Christ in the *Eclogues* (4.5–7), converted him to Christianity, yet Virgil himself did not understand the meaning of the words he wrote. All told Dante's narrative of purgation has dimensions of complex human feeling quite different from those of both *Inferno* and *Paradiso*.

Chapter 6
Politics

> Soleva Roma, che 'l buon mondo feo,
> due soli aver, che l'una e l'altra strada
> facean vedere, e del mondo e di Deo
> [Rome, that made the good world,
> used to have two suns that showed the one way and the other,
> that of the world and that of God]
>
> (*Purg.* 16.106–8)

Recent history

In the letter to Can Grande della Scala, the aim of the *Comedy* is said to be to 'remove those living in this life from a state of misery and bring them to a state of felicity', and the poem is said to belong to the philosophical category of ethics because it is concerned not with speculation but with action. Whether Dante wrote this letter or not, the comment seems a faithful representation of a large part, though by no means the whole, of the *Comedy*'s purpose. By the same token, though the letter does not say so, that purpose can also be said to be political, since for Dante and his time, following a tradition of thought that goes back to Aristotle, politics and ethics were indissolubly connected: political actions must be guided by moral standards, and must enable human beings to live virtuous lives. Thus in the poem the political and the moral merge into one another: moral reflections lead to political conclusions, and political arguments are couched in strongly moral terms. The result, though, is by no means a simple set of general moral exhortations. These are certainly present in the *Comedy* but they emerge from a deep and passionately felt engagement with the political and social realities of the time.

The Florence in which Dante lived until his exile was one of a patchwork of small city-states (*comuni*) that covered northern and central Italy. In the following two centuries it would gradually expand until it controlled almost all of present-day Tuscany, but in Dante's time its territory was tiny by modern standards: nearby Pisa, Siena, Lucca, and Arezzo were also independent city-states, and were Florence's rivals and sometimes adversaries. Yet Florence was also one of the richest and most populous cities in Europe—far larger, for instance, than London. Built originally on wool production and the wool trade, its economy was vastly extended by banking networks that served some of the major European rulers, providing substantial loans and other financial services. Ruled as a free commune, the city went through frequent changes of regime and constitution; in modern terms, however, it was nothing like a democracy. By 1300, the purported date of the journey of the *Comedy*, it was governed by an oligarchy of aristocratic families and members of the manufacturing and commercial guilds supported by a class of officials with legal training, of whom Dante's mentor Brunetto Latini was a prominent representative. Religious foundations, particularly the mendicant orders, played a significant part in social life: the orders' churches, notably Santa Croce, Santa Maria Novella, and Santo Spirito, were prominent features of the city's architectural and cultural landscape; Dante says in the *Convivio* that he gained his philosophical education in their schools. But in principle, if not in practice, the Church and its organizations had no involvement whatever in the actual governance of the city, and the Papacy was a potential and often actual political opponent.

An advanced urban society of this kind was a highly favourable context for the sort of secular view of humanity we have discussed in the last chapter. It had its negative sides, however, and none more so than the factional struggles by which all the Italian city-states were plagued. The different factions of nobles and wealthy merchants that ruled them tended to divide themselves into Guelfs and Ghibellines, respectively the party of the Pope, who ruled the regions immediately to the south of Tuscany, and that of the Holy Roman Emperor, the nominal if not the actual ruler of many of the communes. In Florence in turn, as we said in Chapter 2, the ruling Guelf party split in the late 13th century into the Black and White factions, the division leading to Dante's exile. More than anything else, it was exile that shaped Dante's views on politics and led him, partly driven by personal bitterness and perplexity, to theorize them with a depth, scope, and adventurousness that goes far beyond the thinking of his Florentine contemporaries, and stands out against contemporary orthodoxies elsewhere.

The *Comedy* is filled with references to events in recent Italian history. The factional struggles in Florence are the central topic of one of the most dramatic episodes in *Inferno*, when among the heretics of canto 10 Dante meets the Florentine aristocrat and Ghibelline leader Farinata degli Uberti. Dante, whose family was historically Guelf, is drawn by Farinata into an argument about their rival parties, which Dante wins by pointing out that the Guelfs eventually expelled the Ghibellines from Florence. In riposte, Farinata harks further back to the Battle of Montaperti in 1260, five years before Dante's birth, in which the Florentine Guelfs were defeated by an alliance of Ghibelline forces, and which led to a brief period of Ghibelline domination in Tuscany. As isolated and as strong in life as he seems to be in death, Farinata claims that he alone prevented Florence from destruction by the victorious army. This was an achievement Dante clearly respected, but Farinata is another of *Inferno*'s contradictory human figures. Dante applies to him the Aristotelian epithet *magnanimo*, 'great-souled' (10.73), a term associated with fortitude, dignity, a desire for honour, and a due sense of pride, though in the *Convivio* (1.11) he had also used the word more negatively to indicate vainglorious pride in oneself.

A tapestry of fragmentary stories and allusions in Hell and Purgatory sketches the other stages in the Guelf/Ghibelline struggle and its aftermath. Mosca dei Lamberti, the supposed cause of the factions in Florence, is encountered in the *bolgia* of the sowers of discord in Hell (*Inf.* 28.106–11). The Battle of Benevento in 1266, which marked the effective end of Ghibelline ascendancy in Italy for the remainder of the century, is a major focus of the episode in *Purgatorio* 3 of Manfred, the illegitimate son of Frederick II. This led to a long period of Guelf dominance in Florence, ushered in by the brief rule of two members of the order of *frati godenti*, supposedly politically neutral but suspected of favouring the Guelfs: they are punished in the *bolgia* of the hypocrites (*Inf.* 23). The division of the Florentine Guelfs into the Black and the White factions, which led to Dante's exile in 1302, is foretold by the thief Vanni Fucci (*Inf.* 24), and earlier by the glutton Ciacco (*Inf.* 6), who also alludes to the support given to the Blacks by Dante's arch-enemy, Pope Boniface VIII. Boniface died three years after Dante's journey is supposed to have taken place, but his condemnation in Circle 8 to the *bolgia* of the simoniacs, the sellers of ecclesiastical offices, is revealed in advance by one of his predecessors, Nicholas III (*Inf.* 19).

In *Inferno* it is the particular that dominates, and the negative side of Dante's politics. Hell is eternal but, through the image of their earthly selves that the individual souls embody, it is also a polemical representation of the disastrous state of contemporary politics and society. Throughout the stress falls on individual behaviour: social ills are denounced in terms of personal morality and responsibility, though vice versa sins that might seem more private to us, such as lust or gluttony, are almost always seen in relation to their effects on others. In this way Italian cities are condemned for their corruption one by one. Florence in particular, the 'divided city' (*Inf.* 6.61), is governed by pride, envy, and avarice (*Inf.* 15.61 and 78); new arrivals and sudden wealth have led to pride and excess (16.73–5); the circle of the thieves is notable for Florentine citizens (25.1–11). One after another, Pistoia, the Romagna, Bologna, Siena, Pisa, and Genoa are also singled out and condemned. The strongest attack is directed at the financial corruption of the Church, shown most in the buying and selling of ecclesiastical goods and offices, contrary to the Christian rule of poverty. The popes, Dante says in the *bolgia* of the simoniacs, have made gold and silver their god (19.112–14), inverting Christ's teaching in a way that is grotesquely, even comically, represented by the sinners' punishment, which is to be plunged upside down in burning tombs, with the fires of love that should have inspired them turned into flames rising from the soles of their feet.

Aside from moral diatribes, the general reasons for Italy's contemporary woes are only hinted at in *Inferno*. There is the denunciation of the Donation of Constantine in canto 19 (for which see p. 92), and also, at the very bottom of Hell, an indication of the central importance of the Roman Empire in the description of Satan, whose three mouths are chewing the three worst traitors in history. Together with Judas, these are Brutus and Cassius, the assassins of Julius Caesar, who for Dante was or should have been the first Caesar or Emperor. It is a remarkable equation of the three figures, which clearly leaves no room for consideration of Brutus as a tormented defender of republican freedom, but which makes the fundamental point that betrayal of the Roman Empire goes against God's will as much as does betrayal of Christ. At this stage, however, none of the issues are elaborated, and Dante the character remains unenlightened. Their full significance only becomes apparent to him, and to the reader, in *Purgatorio*, where Dante's moral purification and intellectual enlightenment accompany one another.

Political theory in *Purgatorio* and the *Monarchia*

Condemnations of cities are much less frequent in Purgatory, but they are all summed up in a long diatribe in canto 6, occasioned by the poet Sordello's eager embrace of Virgil when the latter indicates that he is from Mantua, Sordello's native city. That is how fellow citizens should behave. Instead Italy is enslaved by foreign powers, and is not 'the mistress of provinces' (as it was in Roman times) 'but a brothel' (l. 78: 'non donna di province, ma bordello'), its states full of tyrants, at war with each other, and divided by faction. Florence is again the object of particular scorn, this time for its frequent changes of government and institutions. It is in this authorial intervention that Dante outlines, for the first time, the immediate political reason for this corruption and strife and points to its solution. It has arisen because the Emperor is absent, and the Church is seeking to take over the Empire's role. Dante has now touched on the central tenet of his political thinking and of the *Comedy*'s political message.

The full explanation comes on the terrace of the wrathful, in canto 16 of *Purgatorio*, the fiftieth canto of the 100 that make up the *Comedy*, and therefore at its very centre. Dante and Virgil meet an otherwise unidentified Lombard courtier called Marco, with whom Dante raises the general question to which everything said so far about the contemporary world has been leading: is the world empty of all virtue, 'loaded and blanketed with wickedness' (l. 60), because of the action of the stars and therefore providence, or does the fault lie with humanity? Marco's answer is that while the stars influence human behaviour up to a point, it is humans who are at fault. Although the human soul possesses free will and naturally desires what is good, it is liable to misapprehend the true nature of that good and therefore exercise its will wrongly. This is why laws are necessary, to guide the human will, and a political authority is necessary to ensure the laws are obeyed. That authority is now absent, as he says in the lines at the head of this chapter: in earlier centuries the Roman Emperor kept mankind on the right road in this world, while the Pope led mankind to God in the next. Now, however, the Papacy has encroached on the Empire's divinely ordained authority by seeking to rule human affairs in this world. It is this confusion of powers that is the cause of all the strife and corruption that Dante's poem has so far recorded.

This is the political doctrine which Dante expounds in its fullest form in the *Monarchia* (the title means literally 'Government by One'), the three books of which aim in turn to prove three related points: mankind should be governed by a single ruler, that ruler is the Roman Emperor, and the Roman Emperor's authority derives directly from God and not from the Pope. The arguments relate to real political need, evidently, but the question of their practical application is more complex. By Roman Emperor Dante meant the Holy Roman Emperor, who was elected by a college of German princes and who therefore tended to be much more closely tied to Germany than to Italy, although he was the legal suzerain of many northern and central Italian city-states. Under Frederick II, who also ruled as king over southern Italy and Sicily, the Empire was a real political force in Italy. That ceased after Frederick's death in 1250, for none of his immediate successors was formally crowned or took any interest in the peninsula. In the diatribe in *Purgatorio* 6, Dante inveighs against the Emperor Albert I, who ruled at the purported time of the *Comedy*'s journey, for neglecting his duties towards Italy; his predecessor Rudolph is in the section of the negligent rulers in Ante-Purgatory (*Purg.* 7.94–6). All this changed, however, with the election of Henry VII, Count of Luxemburg, as Emperor in 1308. Assuming the throne in 1309, Henry embarked on an expedition to Italy in the following year, to pacify the Italian city-states nominally under his rule, and to receive his crown formally from Boniface VIII's eventual successor, Pope Clement V. After establishing his authority over a number of northern Italian cities, Henry's expedition was successfully resisted by Florence and other states and lost the support of the Papacy. It ended with Henry's death from malaria in 1313 at Buonconvento, near Siena.

Dante responded to Henry's expedition with huge enthusiasm. The most direct evidence of this is in three Latin letters he wrote in 1310–11, to the rulers and peoples of Italy, to the Florentines, and to Henry himself. Using language of sacral intensity, these letters reiterate the principle that had already been outlined in the *Convivio*, that the Emperor is the divinely ordained ruler of Italy and the world. Hence the Italian states must acknowledge his sovereignty, and Florence should abandon its resistance or face destruction. Since the *Monarchia* provides a detailed theoretical justification of Dante's attitude in these letters, and indeed repeats some of their arguments, past scholars tended to assume that it was written in the same period. The consensus now is to accept an explicit reference in Book 1 to canto 5 of *Paradiso* as proof that the treatise was written well after Henry's death. If so, the book was not an immediate response to events, but a systematic statement of the political beliefs to which Dante adhered, in substance, throughout most of his life after exile. Certainly the argument is all in terms of first principles and logic, and has little to say about practicalities.

Book 1 of the *Monarchia* argues, rather abstractly, that mankind needs a single ruler, because its general aim is to realize its collective intellectual potential, and one person is required to direct mankind towards this. The Emperor is thus the best guarantor of human freedom, since freedom means fulfilment through the exercise of reason, and a just government by a single Emperor is the best way of ensuring this. Dante seems to have conceived of the Emperor as a kind of overarching authority above the rulers of individual states with their own laws. Hence, alongside other equally abstract arguments, he puts forward the more practical consideration that a single ruler is required to resolve conflicts between subordinate rulers. A universal ruler will also be the most just possible, because, possessing everything, he will have no desire to increase his power and wealth, an argument that illustrates Dante's essentially optimistic view of human nature, despite the lessons of Roman imperial history.

Why should the Roman Emperor be this single ruler? Dante says he had once been amazed at the Romans' success in conquering the world through force of arms, but now realizes that this was decreed by divine providence and ordained by nature. In Book 2, despite his view that human affairs have gone badly awry in his own time, he develops the argument that, in the longer term, history is willed by God, and the Romans' victories in their wars were God-given, sometimes even the result of miraculous interventions. As we shall see, this providential view of history is further supported in *Paradiso*, with its picture of the essential universal order that underlies the surface chaos on earth. Stressing, contrary again to the evidence of history, the Romans' virtue and desire for the common good, Dante also argues that the Empire's legitimacy is shown in the Bible: Christ recognized the authority of the Emperor in his life on earth, and redeemed humankind by accepting the judgement passed on him by the Emperor's legal representative, Pontius Pilate.

The discussion of the relationship between Emperor and Pope in Book 3 builds on the argument, first put forward in the *Convivio*, that the role of the Emperor is to lead humanity to happiness through the exercise of reason, following the philosophy of Aristotle. The Emperor's authority derives directly from God, as does that of the Pope, but, as the successor of St Peter, the Pope's authority is over the Church, not the world as a whole. Dante refutes arguments based on the document entitled the Donation of Constantine, in which the 4th century Emperor purportedly assigned political authority over the Western Empire to the Pope. He does not question the document's authenticity, but argues that Constantine had no right to make the donation, and the Pope no right to receive it. His most fundamental and radical argument, however, is one we have already encountered in Chapter 3: human beings have two essential parts, the corruptible and the incorruptible; the former is the transient being that lives on earth, the latter the eternal being that takes up residence in Heaven. To these two sides divine providence has assigned the two separate goals of happiness in this life and happiness in Heaven. The Emperor is ordained to lead humans to the first, the Pope to the second—though in a concession which might seem to undermine his argument, Dante concludes by saying that earthly happiness is 'in some sense ordered towards eternal happiness', and so the Emperor should show reverence to the Pope without in any way being subject to him.

Given that the *Comedy* is set in 1300, Dante's hopes for Henry VII and the restoration of imperial authority are necessarily voiced in the form of symbolic or allusive predictions, and we cannot always be sure when he has Henry's expedition specifically in mind. He may be represented in the *veltro* or greyhound who will one day chase the wolf of avarice back into Hell, as Virgil says on their first meeting, though it seems likely that Dante wrote the earlier parts of *Inferno* before Henry's election. For most of Hell and at least two-thirds of Purgatory the accent falls on moral corruption, and there is no hint that Dante sees any positive solution to Italy's ills emerging. Then, in *Purgatorio* 23, Dante's friend Forese Donati foretells the divine punishment about to strike the shameless Florentine women who bare their breasts in public, and the prophecy seems to reflect Dante's warning to the Florentines, in his letter of 1311, of the dangers of resisting the Emperor's mission (*Ep.* 6). But it is in the Earthly Paradise that Dante's hopes of Henry are most evident. This pivotal moment in Dante's journey, when Beatrice appears and when both innocence and human perfection are seemingly recovered, also offers in symbolic form the fullest synthesis and articulation anywhere in the *Comedy* of Dante's political and historic vision.

After entering the Garden of Eden, he sees a procession of figures representing the seven gifts of the Holy Spirit, the Ten Commandments, and the books of the Old and New Testaments. There follows the chariot of the Church, drawn by a gryphon, a being that is half eagle and half lion, representing the twin natures of Jesus as God and man, and surrounded by female figures representing the theological and moral virtues (respectively, faith, hope, and charity, and justice, temperance, fortitude, and prudence). On the chariot rides Beatrice, Dante's beloved, but also at this moment an abstraction, perhaps the Church or Theology, perhaps the Papacy itself, her commanding authority shown by the comparison to an admiral on a ship. We have thus followed, symbolically, the providential design leading from the time of Moses through the Old Testament up to the coming of Christ and the establishment of the Church. After the intense personal exchange between Dante and Beatrice, providential history resumes with a series of allegorical events representing the early persecutions of Christians, heresy, the Donation of Constantine, and Christianity's schisms; then the chariot of the Church turns into the monster and the Babylonian whore of the Apocalypse, now made the strongest representation in the *Comedy* of the degeneration and corruption of the Papacy. A giant appears next to the whore, beats her, and drags her off into the forest, in prophecy of the transfer of the papal seat from Rome to Avignon in 1305 engineered by the King of France, to the horror not just of Dante but of Italians generally (see Figure 8).

Nevertheless, if the message of all this is that human history has reached its nadir, *Purgatorio* still ends on a strongly hopeful note. In the final canto Beatrice prophesies the imminent arrival of a mysterious figure designated by the Roman numeral DXV (515), who will show himself the true heir to the Holy Roman Empire by killing the whore and the giant. DXV may well be a transposition of Latin *dux* ('leader'), and has all the air of referring to Henry VII's forthcoming arrival in Italy and Dante's confident expectation that he will put the French in their place, set the Church to rights, and sort out the conflicts between Italian states.

Politics in *Paradiso*

By the time most of *Paradiso* was written, Henry's expedition had failed, he himself was dead, and Dante's hopes for imminent

8. Gustave Doré, The Whore and the Giant (*Purgatorio* 33). Doré's much-reproduced 19th century illustrations emphasize the dramatic qualities of Dante's text.

change had evaporated. In her final speech in the *Comedy*, Beatrice shows Dante the seat in the ranks of the blessed souls that is reserved for 'l'alto Arrigo' (30.137: 'the lofty Henry'), who will try to set Italy to rights before she is ready. The tone of regret for what has been lost or perverted is characteristic. *Paradiso* is melancholic, though almost as scathing as *Inferno*, about political confusion and malpractice on earth, now seen in canto 19 as extending beyond Italy to a whole range of European kings and princes. In canto 6 there is a condemnation of contemporary factionalism by the 6th century Emperor Justinian, of the Guelfs for opposing the Empire, and of the Ghibellines for using the Empire for their own ends. But Justinian's main subject, as we shall see in the next chapter, is the Empire's providential role. Seen from the perspective of Heaven political issues are not so immediate or painful, and Dante directs his attention more to understanding and appreciating the underlying order of history and of the universe.

Where polemic is heightened and intensified in *Paradiso* is with regard to the Church. Again and again the blessed souls turn vehemently and at length to its abandonment of the principles which it was founded to maintain. The clergy are materialistic and avaricious, indulgences and positions are bought and sold freely, preachers purvey falsehoods, or just try to make their congregations laugh. In the Heaven of the Sun there is a celebration of the lives of St Francis and St Dominic, who both founded reforming monastic orders, calling for a return to a New Testament ethics of religious poverty, precisely such as Dante was proposing for the Papacy of his time; both orders are now as corrupt as the rest of the Church. The most ferocious condemnation of the Papacy comes late in Dante's ascent. In the Heaven of the Fixed Stars, St Peter, the founder of the Catholic Church, launches into a violent diatribe (27.19–66) against his successor at the time of Dante's journey: Boniface VIII is a usurper under whom the Papacy is vacant in the eyes of God, and who has made St Peter's burial place a 'cloaca | del sangue e della puzza' (ll. 25–6: 'a sewer | of blood and stench'). When St Peter stops speaking the whole of Heaven turns red in shame. Nevertheless some optimism remains. St Peter evokes the spectre of the Roman Empire, which divine providence defended in the distant past and will do again. Beatrice echoes him at the end of the same canto, with the prophecy that the current absence of government, which causes all virtuous impulses in the young to be corrupted, will soon be remedied:

'true fruit will come after the flower' (27.148). We do not know if Dante had anything concrete in mind. At one point it might have seemed that Can Grande, the Emperor's representative in Italy in the last years of Dante's life, would achieve great things, but nothing in fact ensued.

Yet in *Paradiso* Dante is also resolutely, even heroically positive with regard to his own position as a political exile, in a way he had never been before. In the Heaven of Mars he meets with his 11th century ancestor Cacciaguida, who had died fighting as a crusader in Palestine. Towards the end of this long encounter, which occupies most of canti 15 to 17, Cacciaguida urges Dante to prepare himself for the exile about to come, predicting the hostility that will develop between him and the other White Guelfs, as a result of which he will become 'a party for yourself' (17.69). He will be poor and dependent on patronage, but political isolation also means that he will rise above factionalism, and be able to speak out, as Cacciaguida urges him, to tell everything that he sees and learns on this journey through the afterlife. It is a destiny which Dante readily embraces, now looking more to readers of the future than to his contemporaries.

Cacciaguida also gives a new historical dimension to Dante's view of contemporary Florence. In his time, he says, Florence was a fifth of its present size, and its population lived without factional strife, 'at peace, sober and chaste' (15.99). Corruption and division came from rapid territorial expansion and the influx of outsiders, which led to damaging racial impurity; the happy harmony was ended by the murder of Buondelmonte de' Buondelmonti in 1215 and the resultant split of the city into Guelfs and Ghibellines. It is not Dante's most engaging moment, but the nostalgic conservatism he voices here underlies his repeated condemnation of contemporary avarice elsewhere. In this respect, history was certainly against him: the economic developments he deplores were the source of Florence's wealth and territorial expansion, and of its leading political and cultural position in the Renaissance.

There are many ways in which Dante's political views lacked realism, particularly in their universal claims. His interests were not European but Italian, though, contrary to his Risorgimento readers, he was no Italian nationalist; European politics are only dealt with in generic moral terms, with the one exception of France, mainly on account of its involvement in Italian affairs culminating in the removal of the Papacy to Avignon. Apart from Germany, the idea of a Roman Emperor had practical consequences only in Italy, and there, after Henry VII's failed mission, it was never to be a significant political reality. Where Dante was truly prophetic, albeit some centuries in advance, was as an early and forceful proponent of the separation of Church and state. This would become in due course a principle central to European political thought and culture, and while Dante's writings played a minor role in future debates on the subject, the Church was not slow to respond to his challenge: in 1327 or a little later, a Dominican friar, Guido Vernani, wrote a polemical refutation of the *Monarchia*, which was subjected to ritual burning around the same period. In the mid-16th century, at the height of the Counter-Reformation, it was placed on the Index of Prohibited Books and remained there until 1900. The *Comedy* was not subjected to such attentions, perhaps because it was written in Italian, and therefore notionally of less interest to the educated clergy; in fact it was tendentially a much more radical rejection of ecclesiastical authority, looking forward to the fundamental Protestant assertion of the freedom and responsibility of the individual conscience. As regards himself, Dante declares again and again that it was God who ultimately revealed to him the truths that he asserted. Mediation by the Church is simply sidelined. As regards the Church's powers on earth, history eventually proved him right, when the army of the new Italian state seized control of Rome from the Papacy in 1870.

Chapter 7
God

Trasumanar significar *per verba*
non si poria
[To go beyond the human cannot be put into words]
                                              (*Par.* 1.70–1)

Beatrice

Paradiso is the most beautiful and demanding of the three parts
of the poem. Dante declares at the start of canto 2 that he is
sailing over a sea that has never been sailed before. Only the few
who really aspire 'al pan de li angeli' (l. 11 'to the bread of the
angels') should set out after him. If we do go on, what we encounter
again and again is Dante's struggle with the impossibility of
expressing the inexpressible, making his readers struggle too.
Heavenly bliss and divine knowledge necessarily exceed the
capacities of human language and understanding. As Dante says
in the striking neologism at the head of this chapter, 'trasumanar',
going beyond the human, cannot be put into words—though he
makes a powerful attempt at doing so. At the same time *Paradiso*
is not all otherworldly, as we have already seen: it remains very
much concerned with the human world that it transcends, and
with the relationship of knowledge of the world below to
knowledge of the world above. These alternating foci of attention
are discussed in terms which post-medieval readers take time to

attune to, and which Dante's earlier readers already required help with, if commentators are anything to go by. Yet the poetic force and beauty of much of the writing are almost immediately graspable. Intellectual discourse merges with astounding visual descriptions rich in lyrical feeling, and expressed in a language which becomes more difficult, as Dante raises the level of the style, but also more expressive and inventive, in ways that go far beyond *Inferno* and *Purgatorio*.

The power of Dante's writing and thought is enough, in most readers' experience, to make them forget about the oddity at the very centre of *Paradiso*, even more than of his work as a whole. Dante is a Christian writer who largely sidelines Christ or, perhaps better, feels he cannot write about him directly. His miracles and teaching are certainly referred to quite frequently, especially in *Purgatorio*. His name is never mentioned in the *Inferno*, though it does appear in *Purgatorio*, and in *Paradiso* it appears in rhyme position only, and rhymes only with itself. Perhaps in accordance with the implied sacred quality of the name, the actual figure of Christ appears only fleetingly. There is a ciphered representation in the gryphon drawing the chariot with Beatrice on it in the Earthly Paradise. Much later, in the Heaven of the Fixed Stars, in what Beatrice identifies as the triumph of Christ, he appears as an intolerably powerful light that Dante spends some lines saying he cannot describe (*Par.* 23.28–69). In the Empyrean he is represented only as one of three circles contained in the light of God, though as we shall see the question of his humanity is at the very centre of the final vision.

Thus for most of *Paradiso*, instead of following Christ, Dante follows Beatrice. She is his guide through the heavenly spheres up into the Empyrean, where she is replaced by St Bernard of Clairvaux, much as she had replaced Virgil in the Earthly Paradise. Her mission accomplished, she resumes her seat in the heavenly hierarchy, and St Bernard, with his greater spiritual powers, leads Dante through the last stage of his journey to the vision of God. Is she still the Florentine woman Dante had loved in life? The strongly personal encounter in the Earthly Paradise had suggested that in some ways she was, and Dante will go back to his first sight of her when he makes his farewell speech to her in *Paradiso* 30. At the same time she is obviously now much more capable, knowledgeable, and spiritual. Dante had reported none of her words directly in the *Vita nova*. In the Earthly Paradise she had spoken to him in no uncertain terms. Now she delivers complex speeches explaining features of their ascent and putting Dante right on various scientific and theological issues, as well as delivering severe judgements on the behaviour of those living in the world below. The lines from *Purgatorio* at the head of Chapter 4 distinguish her area of knowledge (*fede*) from that of Virgil (*ragione*), and her place in the procession of the Earthly Paradise indicates that she also has a role in universal history, though it is impossible to find a satisfactory abstraction that covers all her facets. Faith, Theology, or the Church: any or all of these might seem appropriate at various moments of *Paradiso*, but even here they never quite oust her individuality.

For the human and still limited Dante it is only through focusing on her that his knowledge of the divine beyond her can grow. The process is exemplified in canto 1, when the two of them rise up to the Moon, and Beatrice looks not at Dante but at the Sun and the Heavens above it, while Dante looks at her. That is enough to lift them instantaneously to a higher sphere, and with each ascent the beauty of her eyes and smile increase, each time overwhelming his senses and his powers of expression even more strongly. She remains the object of passionate adoration throughout, but her lover is God: 'O amanza del primo amante, o diva' (*Par.* 4.118: 'O beloved of the first lover [God], o goddess'), Dante says to her in the Heaven of the Moon. Her love for Dante is the result of the love produced by her own contemplation of God, and tends towards the love of a general kind which all the blessed souls that he meets are eager to lavish on him. In that regard Beatrice may, just, be recuperable into Christian orthodoxy.

Heavenly bliss

Dante's view of the nature of heavenly bliss is partly anticipated in Virgil's explanation of sinful tendencies in *Purgatorio*, that these are all the result of erroneous love: love is the desire for the good, which is innate in human beings; the greater the good, the greater the love. The greatest good is God, and all other kinds of good (human beauty, sensual pleasure) are only reflections of the divine; Dante's knowledge of Plato was limited, but in this regard he is a Neoplatonist. Once purified of sinful tendencies, as Dante has been at the end of *Purgatorio*, human souls desire nothing but God; thus Dante rises up from the Earthly Paradise to the heavenly spheres, without effort or any awareness of ascending, drawn towards the Empyrean from which God's light descends by the 'concreata e perpetüa sete | del deiforme regno' (2.19), a powerfully concentrated expression meaning, literally, the perpetual thirst created simultaneously with the human soul for the realm that has the form of God.

As Beatrice explains to Dante in the Primum Mobile, the act of seeing the 'vero in che si queta ogne intelletto' (28.108: 'the truth in which all intellect finds rest') generates love and joy. Heavenly bliss results from the fulfilment of the intellect through knowledge of the ultimate reality in the mind of God, and therefore by the same token from the fulfilment of love. In Heaven we will thus know directly the truths which on earth we can only accept as matters of faith or know only partially through reasoning, the greatest of which is the mystery of the Trinity. A corollary is that different souls enjoy different degrees of bliss according to their merits and hence the depth of their knowledge of God: the more the knowledge, the greater the bliss. The souls all dwell in the Empyrean, but appear to Dante in the different lower heavens in order to illustrate to him their different degrees of beatitude (see Box 5), their brightness and beauty increasing as he progresses from one sphere to the next. But souls enjoy all the bliss of which

Box 5 The moral system and structure of Paradise

Heavens	Categories and events	Figures
1 Moon	Breakers of vows	Piccarda
2 Mercury	Those given to fame and glory	Justinian
3 Venus	Lovers	Charles Martel
4 Sun	Lovers of wisdom	Thomas Aquinas, Bonaventure, Solomon
5 Mars	Crusaders	Cacciaguida
6 Jupiter	The Eagle. Lovers of justice	Trajan, Ripheus, Constantine
7 Saturn	Contemplatives	Peter Damian
8 Fixed Stars	Triumph of Christ, Dante's examination on faith, hope, and charity	Saints Peter, James, and John, Mary, Adam
9 Primum Mobile or Crystalline Heaven	God and the angels as lights around a dazzling point	
10 Empyrean	The Blessed in the Heavenly Rose, the final vision	St Bernard

God

they are capable, and joyfully accept the inequality as God's will: as Forese's sister Piccarda Donati says to Dante in the first sphere, the Heaven of the Moon, 'E 'n la sua volontade è nostra pace' (3.85: 'And in his will is our peace').

This idea of bliss as knowledge is the central feature of the kind of religious belief that Dante represents. It is not peculiar to him, but an accepted part of the scholastic culture to which he subscribed, and a natural consequence of the Aristotelian principle of the primacy of the intellect that we have traced in earlier chapters. Its limitations, which classical philosophers failed to recognize, are evident only on earth: in Heaven, apart from the different degrees of beatitude that different souls enjoy, the only limitation is that the entirety of God's truth is beyond the comprehension of any mind in creation, including the angels. Dante represents himself as ascending further and further into that knowledge and the bliss that accompanies it. Unlike the blessed and the angels, he still has a body and still has to rely on human language. He is therefore himself limited in a way they are not, and at times frustrated in his attempts to understand what he saw. Yet, his stress falls not on dissatisfaction, but on the joys of the enlightenment that does occur, and on the ways in which not understanding becomes a stimulus to learn more about the essential nature of the Universe and the workings of divine providence within it.

As by now we might expect, it is the visual representation of bliss that is most striking. The souls in Paradise are not physically recognizable until Dante reaches the heavenly rose. Concrete realism gives way to an imagery of light, movement, and music, through which the souls express the bliss they all share. As Dante and Beatrice move up through the heavenly spheres, they are surrounded by light as they pause in the heavenly body to which each sphere belongs. But the brightness of the souls that they see, like that of Beatrice's smile, is greater than that of the planets and stars, and increases as the souls' bliss increases from one sphere to the next. Their bliss derives from their contemplation of the divine light in the Empyrean, described by Beatrice as the means by which God makes himself visible to human souls and the angels (30.100), and in their turn they emanate light in proportion to the clarity and depth of their vision of God and the love and joy that this gives rise to. The complex brilliance of these representations of light and their effects on Dante tend to make us forget that it is all ultimately metaphorical. As Beatrice points out, the light of Paradise proper, the Empyrean, is 'luce intellettüal, piena d'amore'

(30.40: 'intellectual light, full of love'), something we can only grasp with our minds.

The souls appear to Dante in different formations as the journey through the spheres progresses. The small group in the Moon is replaced by a larger gathering in Mercury, and in Venus by souls moving in circles at varying speeds according to the degree of their bliss. In the sphere of the Sun they dance in circles around Dante and Beatrice, while in Mars they form a cross, and in Jupiter they assume the shape of an Eagle, speaking through its beak with a single voice. In Saturn they appear as lights moving up and down a golden staircase stretching up to the higher reaches of Heaven. Souls express their bliss by singing in heavenly harmony, and by spinning or dancing. Above all they laugh or smile, the Italian words *ridere* and *riso* that Dante uses signifying something between the more earthy English *laugh* and *laughter* and the somewhat weaker *smile* that translators frequently opt for. Neither alternative quite conveys Dante's image of *riso* as the overpoweringly beautiful expression of intense spiritual joy. At the beginning of canto 27, it becomes universal, when the apostles and saints singing together seemed, says Dante, to be 'un riso | de l'universo' (l. 4).

Indeed the language of *Paradiso* is in general more metaphorical, and makes more conspicuous use of other figurative turns of expression, than was the case before, concrete images often mixing with abstractions in subtly surprising ways. 'Io son la vita di Bonaventura' (12.127: 'I am the life of Bonaventure'), the saint says, movingly designating himself as his life rather than his soul, and others among the blessed do the same. The blessed are jewels, splendours, radiances, fires or flames or torches, raptures, loves, flowers or lilies or roses. In groups they are garlands, crowns, lyres, dances; the apostles and saints are the 'beautiful garden that flowers under the rays of Christ' (23.71–2). Paradise or parts of it are the 'eternal triumph', 'this peace', the 'sweet symphony', the 'marvellous angelic temple'. The biblical and the courtly come together in phrases such as the 'eternal palace', the 'court of Heaven', the 'armies of Paradise', the 'sure and joyful realm', where God is the 'Emperor', and the apostles 'counts'. The most important extended metaphors is that of the rose, deployed to represent the concourse of the blessed contemplating God in the Empyrean: under Beatrice's guidance Dante enters

> Nel giallo de la rosa sempiterna,
> che si digrada e dilata e redole
> odor di lode al sol che sempre verna
> [In the yellow of the sempiternal rose,
> that descends and spreads and is redolent
> with the perfume of praise in the sun of perpetual springtime]
>
> (*Par.* 30.124–6)

It is an almost baroque moment in which innovative Latinisms (such as *sempiterna*, *redole*), and an excess of sound effects, complement a metaphorical representation that seems to delight at its own artifice, but also matches the strange sublimity of the vision it describes.

Some images, especially the similes, make severe demands on the intellect and imagination, as when, over twenty-four lines at the start of *Paradiso* 13, the reader is asked to picture a non-existent combination of constellations in order to visualize the concentric dance of two circles of souls in the Heaven of the Sun. Other similes have the concrete precision and clarity of many in *Inferno* and *Purgatorio*, and similarly relate the experience of the afterlife to that of the world below. The music of the circle of souls around Dante in the Heaven of the Sun is like a chiming clock telling the faithful that it is time for dawn prayers (10.139–48). Beatrice, 'erect and attentive' waiting for the appearance of Christ in the sphere of the stars, is like a bird waiting for the sun (23.1–12). In canto 27 she pales, hearing St Peter's diatribe against the contemporary Papacy, like a virtuous woman who hears about the failings of others, not her own. There is an intense lyricism in such images that can be almost disconcerting. In canto 25 Beatrice watches like a silent bride, as St John joins St Peter and St James like a 'happy maiden' who rises and joins a dance in order to honour the bride, not herself (ll. 103–11); and, in a more literary blurring of conventional gendering, the triumph of Christ in canto 23 is compared to the moon appearing surrounded by stars, the 'ninfe etterne | che dipingon lo ciel per tutti i seni' (23.26–7: 'the eternal nymphs who paint Heaven in all its recesses').

Questions of doctrine

Throughout *Paradiso*, visual representations are interspersed with lengthy doctrinal expositions by Beatrice and other souls, mostly on theological and metaphysical subjects. These are not digressions: they are integrally related to Dante's idea of bliss as knowledge. The initial questions are generally prompted by matters that come up in the narrative, and can sometimes seem peripheral and perplexing: why does the moon have spots? how can broken monastic vows be compensated? was Solomon the wisest man ever to live? But such questions are only the starting point for the development of more fundamental themes, which make up the framework of Dante's all-embracing intellectual vision, finally fulfilled in the last canto of the poem when he looks into the mind of God.

Purgatorio had concluded with the corruption figured in the Apocalyptic monster and the Babylonian whore. In *Paradiso* the emphasis is all on order and harmony, not just in the Heavens but, underlying all the surface disorder, on earth as well. That order is what makes the universe similar to God, Beatrice says in the first canto, initiating a theme that runs through the remainder of the poem, and is movingly reflected in the literal narrative:

> Le cose tutte quante
> hanno ordine tra loro, e questo è forma
> che l'universo a Dio fa simigliante.

> [All things
> have an order between them, and this is the form
> that makes the universe similar to God.]
>
> (*Par.* 1.103–5)

Just as the state and behaviour of the souls in Hell is a
metaphorical image of the contemporary world of the living, so
the blissful harmony of the souls in Paradise figures the essential
underlying order of the universe. In one way or another, most of
the doctrinal passages that follow either elucidate and develop this
idea of order, or are connected with it. That does not mean that
current earthly disorder vanishes from view. It remains a live issue
throughout, as we have seen, and is only ultimately resolved, if it is
resolved, in Dante's final blaze of insight at the end.

This universal order is determined by divine providence, which
leads both human and non-human parts of creation to their
different goals, to different ports, as Beatrice puts it, again in
canto 1, through 'lo gran mar de l'essere' (l. 113: 'the great sea of
being'). She explains how this works in the following canto with her
discourse on moon spots, baffling to Samuel Beckett's early alter
ego, named after the Belacqua of *Purgatorio*, in *More Pricks than
Kicks*. Divine providence transmits its power from the Empyrean,
through the angelic intelligences that rule each of the heavenly
spheres below, down to earth, where it determines the nature of
the different species of creation; the spots on the moon simply
reflect the different 'virtues', or elements of that power as they pass
through. The social implications of this theme are brought out
by Charles Martel, the heir to the Kingdom of Naples whom
Dante meets in canto 8. Because it is human nature to be a citizen,
and because society needs humans to perform different roles,
providence ordains the nature of individuals for different activities
and goals in life. Providence also counteracts heredity; otherwise
humans would always be the same as their forebears. The
implications are conflicting: on the one hand Charles's insistence on
the divinely ordained nature of social roles, and therefore of social

divisions, anticipates the conservatism later voiced by Cacciaguida. On the other hand, the idea that providence counteracts heredity points if anything in the other direction, and connects with the argument in the *Convivio* that nobility comes from individual virtue and not from birth. As in other ways, Dante seems able to entertain both views, leaving the conflict between them unresolved.

With abrupt, sometimes disconcerting movements from the celebration and discussion of heavenly order to fierce denunciation of the disorder of the world of the living, *Paradiso* returns again and again to the question why, given this providential design, the world is in its current state. The fundamental reason had been provided by Marco Lombardo and Virgil in *Purgatorio* 16 and 17; sin is the love of inferior goods, and free will allows human beings to choose whether or not to yield to that love. *Paradiso* expands on this theme of the misuse of free will. In the Heaven of the Moon Beatrice discusses monastic vows and the penalties for breaking them: free will is God's greatest gift to human souls and angels, monastic vows are its willing sacrifice, hence breaching them can never be fully compensated. In canto 8, Charles Martel assigns the decadence of the House of Anjou, and general misrule in the contemporary world, to the culpable abuse of free will, because human beings ignore providential design in their assignment of social roles, for instance making rulers out of individuals not ordained to the part. As Marco Lombardo had already said in *Purgatorio* 16, free will means that the human soul is not determined by astral influences, though it will be affected by them. How the principle of free will is reconcilable with that of God's omniscience is discussed on briefly in *Paradiso* 17 with the argument, familiar to many Christian thinkers, that God's ability to foresee contingent events on earth does not mean they are governed by necessity (ll. 37–42).

There is a connection, though Dante does not elaborate it, between the themes of divine providence and free will and the principle, also expounded in *Paradiso*, of the essential

imperfection of earthly creation. In explaining the reason for the
Redemption, Beatrice distinguishes (7.124–48) between the things
that are created directly by God (the angels, the Heavens, and the
human soul), and on the other hand earthly objects and beings,
created indirectly and therefore subject to corruption and change;
God only creates the matter out of which they are made, and the
astral influences that form them. The point is taken up again in
canto 13, where Thomas Aquinas introduces the idea that the
material of earthly creation is not always wholly suited to the
astral influences that operate upon it, so that these do not always
realize fully the divine intention. Dante does not explain why; nor
does he clarify how the soul can be affected by the imperfections
of the corruptible body in which it is housed. But the idea of the
necessary deficiencies of earthly nature goes some way to account
for humans' propensity to sin.

Rather than with these abstruse issues, it seems that Dante is
more concerned with the ways in which providence can also
engage directly in earthly affairs. The crucial intervention is the
Redemption. Adam was expelled from the Earthly Paradise,
Beatrice explains in canto 7, for not accepting the limits that God
has imposed on the human will. The point is repeated by Adam
himself, when Dante meets him in the Heaven of the Fixed Stars,
that the cause of his expulsion from Eden, and hence that of the
human race, was 'il trapassar del segno' (26.117: 'overstepping the
mark'). There is a clear connection with the fate of Ulysses, who
went beyond the boundary set by the pillars of Hercules, and
with Virgil's criticism in *Purgatorio* of classical philosophers
(3.37–45), who think they can understand everything. Humanity's
redemption from Adam's original sin is initially introduced with
Justinian's account of the Roman Empire in canti 6–7. God did this
by allowing mankind to be punished for the sin in the person of his
son, who was sacrificed on the cross. The Empire's providential role
is shown by the fact that this happened under Roman jurisdiction,
and also because the Empire was then destined to punish the Jews
for their deicide with the destruction of Jerusalem. In killing God

the son the Jews were enacting the divine will; but they had to be punished, as Beatrice states, for the fact that by the same token they were killing God the father.

In canto 6 Justinian explains how the providential mission of the Roman Empire is evident not only in its part in the Redemption, but in the whole course of Roman history. Nor is the Empire the only beneficiary of such guidance. The twin episodes in canti 11 and 12 on the new monastic orders founded by St Francis and St Dominic concern two signal attempts to return the Church to apostolic poverty, as we saw in the last chapter. They show how 'La provedenza, che governa il mondo' (11.28: 'Providence, which governs the world') ordained Francis and Dominic to bring this about. It is this faith in the occasional direct involvement of providence in human affairs that seems to account for Dante's continuing political optimism, his belief that, despite the failure of Henry VII, sooner or later things would be set to rights.

Nevertheless the operations of providence are a cause for questioning as well as celebration and optimism, and on no issue more than that of the exclusion from the Redemption of non-believers. Already raised implicitly in Limbo, the issue is most fully examined in *Paradiso* 19, in the Heaven of Jupiter. Dante is troubled by an unspoken doubt which the eagle, formed by the souls and symbolizing divine justice, articulates for him: how can it be just to condemn to Hell (albeit presumably Limbo) a man born on the banks of the Indus who leads a wholly good life, just because, through no fault of his own, he dies unbaptized and without faith? Given Dante's conviction that it is not necessary to be a Christian in order to be wholly good, the question is an urgent one. The eagle does not answer it: the reason, like many parts of God's mind, is beyond human understanding. Yet the matter is not left to rest there. The discussion that follows raises the related issue of predestination, which for Dante refers simply to the selection of individuals by God for particular ends. Thus the Roman Emperor Trajan and the Trojan Ripheus, both pagans in their lives on earth, are, surprisingly, among the souls that form the eagle, and it is as a result of divine predestination that they are there: the former brought back from Hell to learn about Christ, and the latter (the story may have been Dante's invention) having had the future Redemption revealed to him on earth. Why should they have been saved, and other virtuous pagans condemned to Hell? The question still cannot be answered: the eagle says it only shows how remote predestination is from human understanding (20.130–2). Peter Damian continues the theme in the next canto: the reason why he was predestined to speak to Dante at that point in his journey is hidden deep in the mind of God, and not even the highest of the angels could explain it. More than anywhere else in the *Comedy*, these canti (*Paradiso* 19–21) highlight the underlying tension, and the lack of resolution, between Dante's religious belief and his humanistic faith in reason.

The final vision

All these doctrinal passages in *Paradiso* represent the main elements of the fundamental issue in the universe, as Dante saw it: the relationship between man and God, between the world below and the world above. That issue assumes symbolic form in the culminating moment of the final vision prepared for through the succession of events that follows Dante's entry in canto 22 into the Heaven of the Fixed Stars, from which he looks down to contemplate 'L'aiuola che ci fa tanto feroci' (22.151), the beautiful earthly garden which makes its human inhabitants so ferocious to each other. It is here among the fixed stars that Christ appears, as a brilliant light accompanied by Mary and apostles in a triumphal procession. Here Dante is also examined on the theological virtues of faith, hope, and charity, respectively by the apostles Peter, James, and John. These are the virtues necessary for salvation, and Dante provides a definition of each, thus making himself ready for the visions that follow of Heaven proper, the angels, and the blessed souls. Each of these visions is a partial figuration apparently provided for Dante's benefit, just as the souls of the blessed were introduced to him in the different celestial spheres, not in the Empyrean where they reside.

In the Primum Mobile, in an image that reverses the view of the universe presented so far, God appears as an unbearably bright central point surrounded by circles representing the orders of angels. In Dante's cosmology each of the spheres of Heaven is controlled by an angelic order, the names of which are listed by Beatrice in *Paradiso* 28, and God resides outside the spheres in the Empyrean. Reversing the view is a way of representing the true metaphysical or spiritual relationship between God and creation, and also serves to indicate the provisionality of any attempt to express these ultimate realities. Thus, on Dante's arrival in the Empyrean, when the souls appear to him as flowers in meadows on either side of a divine river of light, and the angels as jewel-like sparks of fire flying backwards and forwards between the light and the flowers, all, Beatrice says, are mere 'shadowy prefaces' of what they really are (see Figure 9):

9. Sandro Botticelli, The River of Light (*Paradiso* 30). A delicate line-drawing, which, like Botticelli's other illustrations to the *Comedy*, cannot but simplify the rich complexities of Dante's poetry.

<blockquote>

Il fiume e li topazi
ch'entrano ed escono e 'l rider de l' erbe
son di lor vero umbriferi prefazi.
[The river and the topazes
that come in and out and the smiling of the greenery
are shadowy prefaces of their truth.]

</blockquote>

(Par. 30.76–8)

When Dante bends to drink from the river, the meadows and the
flowers turn into the heavenly rose, and its vast ring of tiers
encircles the reflection, in the surface of the Primum Mobile, of the
ultimate source of divine light coming from above. But this too is
only a foreshadowing, provided for Dante's benefit, since Heaven
has neither time nor place, and the souls have been temporarily
invested with the earthly bodies that they will assume for all
eternity only after Judgement Day.

Dante

Something of the same necessarily imperfect and provisional
quality attends the vision of God that follows. After the ever
increasing brightness and intensity of the preceding images, the
final vision marks a change of focus. Dante had often stressed how
difficult it was to recall fully what he had seen. Now the act of
remembering, and the difficulty of doing so, both come to the fore.
He can only record what he thinks he saw, and then only partly: like
a man who on waking recalls the feelings produced by a dream, but
not the dream itself, his vision has almost all disappeared, though
its sweetness (*il dolce*) remains in his heart (33.62–3). After gazing
round the circles of the blessed, encouraged by St Bernard, he looks
up directly into the divine light above, and what he thinks he saw is
the scattered pages of the book of the universe, now united with
love in a single volume (ll. 85–7). Substances and accidents and 'il
lor costume' (l. 88: 'their way of behaving') seemed to be conflated
into what he believes was nothing less than the form of the entire
universe, 'la forma universal di questo nodo' (l. 91: 'the universal
form of this knot'), where the knot seems not to be just a problem,
but the binding of everything together in the supreme reality of

God. Gazing further and more deeply, he sees three circles representing the three aspects of the Trinity, in which the circle of God the Son is marked by a human image. Like a geometrician attempting to square the circle, he tries to see how the image of man relates to the divine circle in which it appears, and, unable to achieve this through his own efforts, he is granted a final blaze of insight that brings his vision to an end. What he sees disappears, but Dante's desire and will are now governed by 'l'amor che move il sole e l'altre stelle' (33.145: 'the love that moves the sun and the other stars'). It is an amazingly confident claim for any poet. It is also wholly in keeping with everything we have learnt about Dante, that love and the effort of understanding should at this final moment go hand in hand.

Dante's journey thus concludes with a vision of the great mystery that lies beyond the reach of earthly reason. But with its focus on the image of God the Son, the significance of the ending is more than a reiteration of theological dogma; it is also concrete and personal. Dante's struggle to understand how the image of man relates to the circle representing God is a final formulation of the major tension that runs throughout his work, between the human and the divine, this world and the next. The blaze of insight at the end seems to have resolved the tension for him; for modern readers, it remains one of the great fascinations of his work. Perhaps in a different way it is resolved for us too. By bringing into the *Comedy* everything of interest to him in the universe he knew, Dante achieves a poetic synthesis in which intellect and imagination constantly merge and separate, giving both the feeling of completion and the sense that there is still something essential that ultimately can only be pointed to.

Further reading

Translations

Divine Comedy

The three-volume bilingual editions by Robin Kirkpatrick (Penguin, 2006–7) and Robert and Jean Hollander (Random House/Anchor Books, 2003–8) have extensive notes and introductions. Clive James's one-volume rhyming version (Picador, 2013) is highly readable and forceful, but idiosyncratic. Other notable modern versions: Dorothy L. Sayers and Barbara Reynolds (Penguin, 1949, 1963); Steve Ellis, *Hell* (Chatto and Windus, 1994); Mark Musa (Penguin, 1984–6); J. G. Nichols (Alma, 2012).

Other works

Vita nuova, tr. Anthony Mortimer (One World, 2011); *Vita nova*, tr. Andrew Frisardi (Northwestern UP, 2012).

Rime, tr. J. G. Nichols and Anthony Mortimer (One World, 2009); Kenelm Foster and Patrick Boyde, *Dante's Lyric Poetry* (Cambridge UP, 1967).

Monarchy, tr. Prue Shaw (Cambridge UP, 1996).

The Banquet [*Convivio*], tr. Christopher Ryan (Stanford, 1989); *Dante's Il convivio (The Banquet)*, tr. Richard Lansing (Garland, 1990).

De vulgari eloquentia, tr. Steven Botterill (Cambridge UP, 1996).

Dantis epistolae, ed. and tr. Paget Toynbee (Oxford UP, 1920).

Critical studies

General

Critical assessments: T. S. Eliot, *Dante* (Faber, 1929); Harold Bloom, 'The Strangeness of Dante', in *The Western Canon* (Harcourt Brace, 1994).

Re-readings: Jeremy Tambling, *Dante and Difference: Writing in the Commedia* (Cambridge UP, 1988); Teodolinda Barolini, *The Undivine Comedy: Detheologizing Dante* (Princeton UP, 1992).

Short general introductions: George Holmes, *Dante* (Oxford UP, 1980); Robin Kirkpatrick, *Dante: The Divine Comedy* (Cambridge UP, 1987); Peter Hawkins, *Dante: A Brief History* (Blackwell, 2006); Nick Havely, *Dante* (Blackwell, 2007); Prue Shaw, *Reading Dante: From Here to Eternity* (Norton, 2014).

Essay collections: Rachel Jacoff (ed.), *The Cambridge Companion to Dante* (Cambridge UP, 1993); Theodore J. Cachey (ed.), *Dante Now* (University of Notre Dame Press, 1995).

Reference: Richard Lansing (ed.), *The Dante Encyclopedia* (Garland, 2000).

Biographical studies: Stephen Bemrose, *A New Life of Dante* (Exeter UP, 2000); Robert Hollander, *Dante: A Life in Works* (Yale UP, 2001); Barbara Reynolds, *Dante: The Poet, the Political Thinker, the Man* (I. B. Tauris, 2006); A. N. Wilson, *Dante in Love* (Atlantic, 2011).

Specific aspects

Politics: Charles T. Davis, *Dante's Italy and Other Essays* (Pennsylvania UP, 1980); J. R. Woodhouse (ed.), *Dante and Governance* (Oxford UP, 1997).

Thought: Edward Moore, *Studies in Dante*, 4 vols. (Oxford UP, 1896–1917: repr. 1968–9); Étienne Gilson, *Dante and Philosophy* (P. Smith, 1968: tr. from French); Kenelm Foster, *The Two Dantes and Other Essays* (Darton, Longman and Todd, 1977); Patrick Boyde, *Dante, Philomythes and Philosopher* (Cambridge UP, 1981), *Perception and Passion in Dante's Comedy* (Cambridge UP, 1995), *Human Vices and Human Worth in Dante's Comedy* (Cambridge, 2000); Elena Lombardi, *The Wings of the Doves: Love and Desire in Dante and Medieval Culture* (McGill, 2012).

Predecessors: Alison Morgan, *Dante and the Medieval Other World* (Cambridge UP, 1990); Teodolinda Barolini, *Dante's Poets: Textuality and Truth in the Comedy* (Princeton UP, 1984); John C. Barnes and

Jennifer Petrie (eds.), *Dante and his Literary Predecessors* (Four Courts, 2007).

Allegory: Charles Singleton, *Dante's Commedia: Elements of Structure* (Johns Hopkins UP, 1997); Robert Hollander, *Allegory in Dante's Commedia* (Princeton UP, 1969).

Poetic technique: Glauco Cambon, *Dante's Craft* (Minnesota UP, 1969); David Robey, *Sound and Structure in the Divine Comedy* (Oxford UP, 2000); John Barnes and Michelangelo Zaccarello (eds.), *Language and Style in Dante* (Four Courts, 2013).

Reception: Paget Toynbee, *Dante in English Literature from Chaucer to Cary c.1380–1844* (Methuen, 1909); Michael Caesar (ed.), *Dante: The Critical Heritage* (Routledge, 1989); Nick Havely (ed.), *Dante's Modern Afterlife* (Macmillan, 1998); Peter Hawkins and Rachel Jacoff (eds.), *The Poets' Dante: Twentieth-Century Responses* (Farrar, Straus and Giroux, 2001); Simon Gilson, *Dante and Renaissance Florence* (Cambridge UP, 2005); Nick Havely, *Dante's British Public: Texts and Readers from the Fourteenth Century to the Present* (Oxford UP, 2014).

Studies of minor works: Patrick Boyde, *Dante's Style in his Lyric Poetry* (Cambridge UP, 1971); Charles Singleton, *An Essay on the Vita nuova* (Cambridge UP, 1949).

On-line resources: Princeton Dante Project (<http://etcweb.princeton.edu/dante/>).

Note on editions used

All quotations from *Divine Comedy* are from *La Commedia secondo l'antica vulgata*, edited by Giorgio Petrocchi (Le Lettere, 1994).

For other works we have taken account particularly of the following editions: Guglielmo Gorni, *Vita nova* (Einaudi, 1996); Gianfranco Contini, *Rime* (Einaudi, 1970); Prue Shaw, *Monarchia* (Le Lettere, 2009); Marco Santagata, *Rime. Vita nova. De vulgari eloquentia* in Dante, *Opere*, vol. 1 (Mondadori, 2011); Manlio Pastore Stocchi, *Epistole, Ecloge, Questio de situ et forma aque et terre* (Antenore, 2012); Gianfranco Fioravanti and Claudio Giunta, *Convivio* in Dante, *Opere*, vol. 2 (Mondadori, 2011); Claudia Villa, *Epistole, Monarchia, Egloge, Questio de aqua et terra, Il fiore, Detto d'amore* in Dante, *Opere*, vol. 3 (Mondadori, 2011).

Index

A

Abelard, Peter 67
absolution 79
abstinence 66
accent 53
acedia 80
Adam 81, 110
Aeneas 68
Aeneid 37, 54–6, 68
Albert I, Emperor 90
Alì 72
Alighieri, Antonia 16
Alighieri, Jacopo 16
Alighieri, Pietro 16, 33
Alighiero 16
allegory 9, 22, 33–43, 55, 81,
     see also literal sense
Almagest 29
anagoge and anagogical 34, 36
angels 41–2, 51, 80–1, 104, 108–10,
     112–13
Ante-Purgatory 78, 90
Apocalypse 94, 107
apostles 105–6, 112
Aquinas, St Thomas 45, 65, 110
Arabs 65
Arezzo 13, 49, 85
Argenti, Filippo 75

aristocracy and aristocrats 16, 76,
     85–6
Aristotle 45, 65–9, 71–2, 76, 82,
     84, 92, 104
Arnaut Daniel 44, 54
astrology 70, 89, 109
Augustine, St 19, 21, 27
Auschwitz 1
avarice and avaricious 24, 69, 80,
     88, 96
Averroes 72
Avicenna 72
Avignon 94, 98

B

bankers and banking 16–17, 48, 85
Banquet, see *Convivio*
Bardi, Simone de' 17
barrators and barratry 17, 74
Batten, John 6
beatitude 17, 64, 102, *see also* bliss
Beatitudes 63, 81–2
Beatrice 3, 11, 15–16, 19–25, 32,
     38–9, 41, 48–9, 51, 68, 80, 82–3,
     93–6, 99–113
Beckett, Samuel 108
Belacqua 83, 108
Benevento 87

Benigni, Roberto 58
Benvenuto da Imola 16
Bernard of Clairvaux, St 39, 100–1, 114
Bertran de Born 73
bestiality 69, 73
betrayal, *see* treachery
Bible 32, 34–7, 38, 45, 57, 59, 67, 81, 92, 105
biography of Dante 16
Blacks, *see* Whites and Blacks
blasphemy 7, 75
blessed 29, 63, 95–6, 101, 104–6, 112–14
bliss 99, 102–7, *see also* beatitude
Boccaccio, Giovanni 12, 16, 33, 41
Boethius 19
bolgia 69, 74, 87–8
Bologna 33, 88
Bonagiunta da Lucca 48–9
Bonaventure, St 105
Bonconte da Montefeltro 78
Boniface VIII 17, 23, 79, 87, 90, 96
Botticelli, Sandro 113
Brunetto Latini 5–9, 15, 32, 44, 46, 75–6, 85
Brutus 74, 88
Buonconvento 90
Buondelmonte de' Buondelmonti 97

C

Cacciaguida 15, 97, 109
Caetani, Michelangelo 31
Caiaphas 72
Campaldino 78
Can Grande della Scala 15, 18, 35, 37, 55, 84, 97
cantica 62–3, 81–3
canto 61–2
canzone 26, 48, 51, 53
Capaneus 75
Cary, Henry 63
Casentino 15, 26

Cassius 74, 88
catharsis 76
Cavalcanti, Guido 15, 17, 50
charity 21, 38, 94, 112
Charles de Valois 17
Charles Martel 108–9
Charon 74
Chaucer 76
Christ 24, 30, 32, 36, 71–2, 74, 83, 88, 92–3, 100, 107, 112
chronology 30–2
Church 9, 24, 45, 57, 78, 85, 88, 90–8, 101, 111
Ciacco 87
Cicero 45, 69, 71
Cino da Pistoia 51
citizens 5, 88–9, 108
city-states 85–6, 90
classicism and classics 1, 5, 8–9, 54–61, 68, 74, 81, 104, 110
Clement V 90
clergy 96, 98, *see also* Church
comedìa 55
comedy and comic style 46, 52, 55, 57, 88
commentaries and commentators 9, 16, 33, 36, 40–1, 43, 55, 73, 100
communes (*comuni*) 85–6
composition 50
conservatism 97, 109
Constantine (Emperor) 88, 92, 94
contemplation 101, 104, 106
contrapasso 73
Convivio 11–13, 15, 18, 21–7, 34, 36, 46–7, 50–1, 54, 65–8, 85, 87, 92
cornice 32
corruption 17, 24, 36, 42, 88–9, 90, 93–4, 96–7, 107, 110
cosmology 29, 30, 113
Counter-Reformation 98
courts and courtliness 21, 52, 72, 106
creation 7, 47, 71, 104, 108, 110, 113
criticism (on Dante) 9, 10, 55, 57

crucifixion 73
Crusades 72
crystalline heaven, see *Primum Mobile*

D

Damian, St Peter 112
damnation 2, 7, 32, 41, 72, 78
dancing 63, 105–6
De vulgari eloquentia 13, 21, 45, 47, 50–6, 61
deicide 110
democracy 85
desire 20–1, 24, 40, 52, 60, 66, 71–2, 78, 80, 82, 87, 89, 91–2, 102, 115
Detto d' amore 14
devils 56–7, 74
dialect 45–6, 54
Diomedes 3, 4
Divine Comedy (title) 55
dolce stil novo 15, 48–50, 54
Dominic, St 67, 96, 111
Dominicans 98
Donati, Corso 17
Donati, Forese 26, 52, 83, 93
Donati, Gemma 16–17
Donati, Piccarda 103
Donation of Constantine 88, 92, 94
donna pietosa 20, 22, 35
'Donne ch'avete intelletto d'amore' 48–50, 53
Doré, Gustave 95
dreams 25, 63, 114
DXV 94

E

Eagle 105, 111–12
earth 29, 72
earthliness 33, 38, 42, 67, 78, 82–3, 87, 92–3, 95, 98, 102, 104, 107–10, 112, 114–15

Earthly Paradise 24, 30, 32, 37, 81, 100–1, 110, *see also* Eden
Easter 30, 81
Eclogues (of Dante) 18
economy 85, 97
Eden 81, 110, *see also* Earthly Paradise
editions (of Dante's works) 119
elegy and elegiac style 52
Elijah 59
Eliot, T. S. 10, 54
Elisha 59
Ellis, Steve 63
Emperor and Empire 17, 38, 45, 67, 74, 78, 86, 88–98, 110–11
Empyrean 29, 100, 102, 104, 106, 113
enjambement 62
enlightenment 2, 19, 38–9, 88, 104
Enlightenment, the 67
envy 80, 88
Epistles (of Dante) 13, 35, 45, 91
Equator 2, 30
Erichtho 69
ethics 5, 25, 51, 66–8, 82, 84, 96
Ethics (of Aristotle) 66–9
Europe 27, 72, 85, 96, 98
Eve 81
Everyman 39
excommunication 78
exegesis 34, 35
exile 2, 5, 8, 12–13, 16–19, 23, 25, 27, 45, 49, 86, 87, 91, 97
existentialists 75
eyes 29, 60, 101

F

fable 34
factions 17, 76, 86–7, 89, 96, 97
faith 38, 65, 68, 72, 94, 101–2, 111–12
false counsellors 59, 70, 76
Farinata degli Uberti 76, 86–7

Index

fede, see faith

felicity 84

fiction 22, 37

figura 36

figurative meanings 33, 105, 112

film-makers 9

Fiore, Il 13, 26, 52

Fixed Stars 29, 96, 100, 110, 112

Florence and Florentines 5, 7, 13, 15–18, 23, 33, 46, 58, 67, 83, 85–8, 93, 97, 101

fortitude 87, 94

France 18, 94, 98

Francesca da Rimini 40–1, 60, 75

Francis, St 67, 96, 111

frati godenti 87

fraud and fraudulent 2–3, 33, 59, 69, 71, 73, 75, *see also* false counsellors

Frederick II 78, 87, 90

French 5, 44, 46, 60

friends and friendship 5, 16–17, 20, 26, 42, 48, 50–1, 82–3, 93

G

Ganges 30

Gemini 15

Genoa 88

gentilezza 50

geography 29–30

Gerione 33

Germany 90, 98

Ghibellines, *see* Guelfs and Ghibellines

Giacomo da Lentini 49

Giants 74

Gibraltar 30

Giovanni del Ponte 12

Giovanni del Virgilio 18

gironi 69, 70

gluttony 26, 69

gods 69, 72

good, the 80–1, 92, 102, 109

grace 7, 24, 36, 38, 41, 79

gramatica 47

greed 66, 80

Greek 34, 44

gryphon 93, 100

guardians 63, 74

Guelfs and Ghibellines 14, 17, 78, 86–7, 96–7

Guido da Montefeltro 76, 79

Guido Novello da Polenta 18

guides 24, 39, 68, 80, 82, 100

guilds 17, 85

Guinizelli, Guido 50, 54

Guittone d'Arezzo 48–9, 51

H

happiness 37–8, 66–7, 82, 92–3

harmony 97, 105, 107–8

Heaney, Seamus 76

heavens 29, 37, 81, 92, 102–4, 110, 113

Hell (structure) 68–72

hendecasyllable 52–3, 55

Henry II of England 73

Henry VII of Luxemburg 17, 90–1, 93–5, 98, 111

heredity 108

heretics and heresy 71–2, 94

Homer 2, 3

homosexuals 6, 7

hope 38, 41, 71–2, 94, 112

humility 66

hypocrites 72, 87

I

imagination 3, 9, 39, 43, 106, 114

incontinence 69–71

incorruptibility 92

individuality 7, 25, 27, 35, 38–9, 40, 42, 79, 82–3, 87, 98, 101, 108–11

indulgences 96

Indus 111

inspiration 24, 49, 50, 54
intellect (*intelletto*) 26, 39, 42–3, 46, 54, 66, 88, 91, 100, 102, 104–7, 115
intelligences 108, *see also* angels
interpretation, *see* allegory
Islam 73
Israel 35
Italy and Italians 17–18, 45, 51–2, 85–98
Italian language 51–3, 57, 60, 62, 105

J

James, St 107, 112
James, Clive 63
Jerusalem 30, 110
Jesus, *see* Christ
Jews and Judaism 73, 110–11
John, St 107, 112
Jubilee 23
Judas 74, 88
Julius Caesar 88
Jupiter 29, 75, 105, 111
justice 37, 74, 75, 94, 111
Justinian 96, 110–11

L

language(s) 9, 10, 13, 32–4, 39, 43–8, 50–2, 55–7, 60, 62–3, 91, 99, 100, 104–5
Latin 13, 18, 20, 35, 44–7, 51, 57, 60, 65, 91, 94
latinisms 57, 106
laughter, see *riso*
laws 89, 91
lecturae Dantis 16
leopard 24
letters (of Dante), see *Epistles*
Levi, Primo 1
light 32–3, 41, 81, 83, 100, 102–7, 112–14
Limbo 72, 111

lion 24
literal sense 34, 36–7, 43, 107, *see also* allegory
Livres dou Tresor 5–6
Lombardy 46
Longfellow, Henry Wadsworth 63
love 7–8, 11–13, 19–22, 34, 37–8, 40–1, 44, 48, 50–1, 68, 71, 80–1, 83, 88, 101–5, 114–15
love-poetry 11–13, 18–22, 27, 37, 40–1, 44, 46, 48, 50–4, 57, *see also* lyric
Lucan 37
Lucca 85
Lucifer, *see* Satan
Lucy, St 23, 38
lust 24, 40–1, 66, 69, 73, 80
lyric and lyricism 9, 11, 45, 52–3, 62, 83, 100, 106–7, *see also* love-poetry

M

magnanimo 86–7
Malacoda 56–7
Malaspina, Currado 15, 42
Malebolge 69, 71–4
malice 69
Manfred 87
mankind 38–9, 67, 90–2, 110
Mantua 89
manufacturing 85
manuscripts 4, 61
Marco Lombardo 89–90, 109
Mars 29, 97, 105
Mary, *see* Virgin Mary
Matelda 42
matter 74, 110
meaning, levels of, *see* allegory *and* literal sense
medieval, *see* Middle Ages
Mediterranean 2
mendicants 85
merchants 16, 48, 85–6

Mercury 29, 105
Metamorphoses 34
metaphor 43, 60–1, 104–6, 108
metaphysics 7, 68, 107, 113
Metaphysics (of Aristotle) 66
metre 52, 61, 63
Middle Ages 8–9, 22, 27, 30, 35–6,
   47, 54, 60, 62, 65, 68, 73
Milton, John 58
Minos 74
miracles 100
moderation 66
modernism 8–10
Muhammad 72
monastic orders 67, 85, 87, 96
Monarchia 13, 37–8, 45, 65, 67,
   89–93, 98
money 7, 15–16
monks 67, 96
monsters 33, 94, 107
Montaperti 86
Moon 29, 42, 101, 103, 105, 107–9
moral philosophy, *see* ethics
Mosca de' Lamberti 87
Moses 94
mother-tongue, *see* vernacular
murderers 70
music 32, 34, 46, 54, 104, 106
myth 34

N

Naples 108
nature 1, 6–7, 32, 47, 68–9, 83,
   91–2, 108, 110
Nazism 1
negligent, the 78, 90
neologism 57, 99
Neoplatonist 102
Nicholas III 87
nobility 50–1, 66, 86, 109
non-believers 111
notaries 48
novelle 46
numbers 20

O

occhi, *see* eyes
oligarchy 85
omniscience 109
order 7, 46, 63, 71, 80–1, 92–3, 96,
   107–9
originality 9, 27, 43, 56
Orpheus 34, 35
Ovid 34
Oxford 18

P

pagans 34, 56, 68, 69, 71–2, 80,
   111–12
pageant 24
Paolo and Francesca, *see* Francesca
   da Rimini
Papacy and Popes 17, 34, 38, 67,
   78–9, 85–93, 106
Paradise (structure) 102–3
pargoletta 25–6
Paris 18, 68
passions 19, 40, 61, 73, 85, 101
penance and penitents 7, 32,
   76–83
perfectibility 80
periphrasis 20, 59–60
personification 34–5, 60
Peter, St 92, 96, 106–7, 112
Petrarch 2, 28
philosophy 1, 9, 11, 15, 22, 35, 43,
   68–9, 72, 84–5, 92, 104, 110
Pier della Vigna 59, 75
Pilgrim's Progress 35
Pillars of Hercules 110
Pisa 76, 85
Pistoia 88
planets 29, 33, 104
Plato 102
plurilinguismo 57
Plutus 74
poema 56
poesia giocosa 52, 56

Poetics (of Aristotle) 76
poetry 10, 13, 19, 21, 35, 37, 40, 43, 45–6, 48–56, 61–2, 69, 83, 113
polysemous 34–5, 43
Pontius Pilate 92
Popes, *see* Papacy and Popes
Portinari, Bice 16
Portinari, Folco 17
Pound, Ezra 54
preachers 96
predestination 111–12
Pre-Raphaelites 49
pride 24, 80, 88
Primum Mobile 29, 102, 113, 114
Priori 17
prodigality 71, 80
prophecy 27
prosopopoeia 35
Protestant 98
Provençal 44, 46, 60–1, 73
providence 37, 89, 92–3, 96, 104, 108–11
prudence 94
Ps 80–1
Psalms 35
Ptolemy 29
punishment 2–3, 32, 40–1, 73, 76, 88, 93, 110–11
purgation 76–83
Purgatory (structure) 30, 76–83
purification 30, 32, 60, 88
pusillanimous, the 70, 75

Q

Quaestio de aqua et terra 13, 18, 45

R

Ragione, see reason
Ravenna 16, 18
realism 32, 56–7, 59, 61, 63, 104
reason 19–20, 24, 38, 40, 42, 65–9, 71–4, 80, 82, 91–2, 101–2, 112, 115

reception (of the *Comedy*) 9–10
Redemption 36, 110–12
Renaissance 1, 5, 28, 57, 97
repentance 7, 19, 78–9
resurrection 30
Reynolds, Barbara 63
rhetoric and rhetoricians 5, 11, 18, 33, 45, 54, 60
rhyme 21, 50, 60–3, 100
rhythm 54, 62, 80
riches, *see* wealth
Rime 21, 25–6, 48, 50
rime petrose 21
Ripheus 111
riso 105
Risorgimento 9, 27, 98
robbers 70
Romagna 88
Roman de la Rose 13, 26, 35
Roman history 45, 91–3, 110–11
romance languages 46
romances 40, 44, 46
Romantics 27
Rome 17, 45, 84, 94, 98
Rose, Heavenly 106, 114
Rossetti, Dante Gabriel 49
Rudolph, Emperor 90
Ruggieri, Archbishop 76–7

S

sacrifice 109–10
Saladin 72
salvation 24, 38, 72, 78–9, 112
Sartre, Jean-Paul 75
Satan 30, 73–4, 88
Saturn 29, 105
Sayers, Dorothy 63
scholarship (on Dante) 9, 16, 39, 43, 51, 57, 61, 91
scholasticism 9, 13, 45, 103
scripture, *see* Bible
secularism 66–7, 86
senses, *see* allegory
sentence-breaks 62

sermons 46, 81
serpent 41-2, 73
Shakespeare 10, 57
Sicilian School 48-9
Sicily 46, 90
Siena 85, 88, 90
sight, *see* eyes
similes 56, 58-60, 106
simoniacs 34, 87, 88
sins and sinners 19, 23-6, 32, 34, 36, 40, 63, 69, 72-6, 78-81, 87-8, 102, 109, 110
sloth 60, 80
sodomy 6-7
Solomon 107
Song of Songs 37
sonnet 13, 26, 49, 52, 61
soothsayers 75
Sordello 41, 46, 89
soul, nature of 67-8, 87, 89, 102, 104-5, 109-10, 114
sowers of discord 72-3, 87
speculation 68, 84
stars, *see* astrology
Statius 78, 83
stilnovo, see *dolce stil novo*
styles, levels of 51-4, 100
suicides 59, 73, 75
Sun 29, 96, 101, 105-6
sweetness, *see dolce stil novo*
syllables 53
symbols and symbolism 21, 24, 112
syntax 54, 61, 63

theology and theologians 8, 21, 24, 34-5, 38, 94, 101, 107, 115
trade 16, 85
tragedia 85
tragedy and tragic style 52, 55-6, 76
traitors and treachery 69, 73-4, 76, 88
Trajan 111
translations and translators 63-4, 105
trasumanar 99
treachery, *see* traitors and treachery
Tresor, see *Livres dou Tresor*
Trinity 20, 61, 68, 102, 115
triumph 20, 100, 105, 107, 112
troubadours 44, 73
Troy and Trojans 1-2, 111
Tuscany 17, 86

U

Ugolino della Gherardesca 76-7
Ulysses 1-5, 8-9, 32, 68, 75-6, 110
Umbria 46
unbaptized children 72
unbelievers 72, 111
Unification of Italy 9, 98
universities 45, 68
unrepentant, the 7, 32
usury 7

T

Tasso, Torquato 62
temperance 94
terza rima 55, 61-3
terzina 62
Testament, New 36, 66-7, 82, 93, 96
Testament, Old 36, 93-4
theft and thieves 73, 88

V

Vanni Fucci 87
veltro 93
Venice 18
Venus 29, 57, 105
vernacular 44-5, 47-8, 51
Vernani, Guido 98
Verona 6, 15-16, 18, 33
versification 53

vice, *see* sins and sinners
violent and violence 6, 69, 71
Virgil 3–6, 23–6, 30, 32–3, 37–8,
    40, 45, 54–7, 59, 68–9, 71–5, 78,
    80–3, 89, 93, 100–2, 109–10
Virgin Mary 23, 38, 112
virtue 1, 3, 38, 42, 63, 66, 71–2, 76,
    81, 89, 92, 94, 108–9, 112
Visconti, Giovanna 42
Visconti, Nino 42
visions 20, 23, 30, 39, 100–1, 104,
    106–7, 112–15

Vita nova 11, 13, 16, 18–27, 34–5,
    46, 48–51, 101
vocabulary 50, 54–5, 57
volgare, see vernacular
Vulgate 45

W

wealth 74, 85, 91, 97
Whites and Blacks 17, 86, 87, 97
wolf 24
wrath and wrathful 66, 71, 80

Index

SOCIAL MEDIA
Very Short Introduction

Join our community

www.oup.com/vsi

- Join us online at the official Very Short Introductions **Facebook** page.
- Access the thoughts and musings of our authors with our online **blog**.
- Sign up for our monthly **e-newsletter** to receive information on all new titles publishing that month.
- Browse the full range of Very Short Introductions online.
- Read **extracts** from the Introductions for free.
- Visit our library of **Reading Guides**. These guides, written by our expert authors will help you to question again, why you think what you think.
- If you are a teacher or lecturer you can order inspection copies quickly and simply via our website.